THE BEST OF SHENANDOAH NATIONAL PARK

A Guide to Trails and the Skyline Drive

A Tag-Along Book
by Russ Manning and
Sondra Jamieson

Mountain Laurel Place
Norris, Tenn.

Copyright © 1997 by Russ Manning and Sondra Jamieson.

Printed on recycled paper.

Printed in the United States of America.

ISBN 0-9625122-8-1

Front Cover: Crescent Rock
Back Cover: Skyline Drive

Published by

    Mountain Laurel Place
    P.O. Box 3001
    Norris, TN 37828
    (423/494-8121)

for Daniel

Contents

Central District

South District

Acknowledgments

We are grateful to the National Park Service staff at Shenandoah National Park for their support in the preparation of this book. We especially appreciate the support and encouragement of Karen Michaud, Interpretation and Education Leader, and are grateful for her help in guiding the draft manuscript through the review process.

We thank the NPS staff who reviewed the manuscript: Reed Engle, Cultural Specialist, and Robbie Brockwehl, Concessions Specialist, for the introductory sections; Steve Bair, Resource Management Specialist, and Barb Stewart, District Interpreter, for the North District; Rolf Gubler, Resource Management Specialist, and Paul Pfenninger, District Interpreter, for the Central District; and Shawn Green, Resource Management Specialist, and Marsha McCabe, District Interpreter, for the South District. Thanks to Janice Pauley, Park Ranger, for supplying information on horseback riding.

We are also grateful to Greta Miller, Executive Director of the Shenandoah Natural History Association, for meeting with us in the early planning stages.

Shenandoah

Ridge and Valley

When we first began our exploration of Shenandoah National Park we thought this might not be one of our favorite parks. It's a linear park after all, a narrow preserve where you're never really away from it all. It has a road through the middle of it. And nearly all the views from the mountaintops are not of wilderness but of civilization in the surrounding valleys and foothills.

But now we have to unabashedly say we love this place. Because of the easy accessibility of the trails from Skyline Drive. Because of the wonderful views of the Shenandoah Valley to the west and the Piedmont foothills to the east with their rolling farm-lands, rustic inns and bed & breakfasts, wineries, and small towns and communities with their history and independence. And finally, because of the wilderness of the national park itself--official wilderness as it turns out--nearly 80,000 acres designated in 1976. But also wilderness in actuality--forest that has been reclaimed, cascading streams and falls of water, deep canyons and isolated hollows, and the return of the animals--deer, bear, bobcat, grouse, and more that we've seen while hiking the trails.

The park contains 500 miles of trails that take you to sum-mits along the Blue Ridge, ranging up to Hawksbill, the highest at 4050 feet. You'll wander by falls of water: the tallest, Overall Run, at 93 feet; then upper Whiteoak at 86 feet and South River at 83 feet. But also don't miss the falls of Lewis Spring, Dark Hollow, Rose River, Doyles River, Jones Run, and Cedar Run.

Ultimately, this is a park of views. You'll find 70 overlooks scattered along the length of Skyline Drive and numerous other views of hollows and valleys along the trails--from the summits of Mount Marshall and Pass Mountain in the north, from Stony Man and Hawksbill and Marys and Bettys Rocks in the central portion, and from Hightop and Blackrock and Calvary Rocks in the south. We guide you to all of these in this best of Shenandoah National Park.

Norris, Tenn.

Russ Manning and
Sondra Jamieson

Park History

In October 1886, a sixteen-year-old George Freeman Pollock came to the Blue Ridge Mountains of Virginia to explore his father's land. Pollock's father was one of several principal stockholders in the Miner's Lode Copper Company that controlled the 5,371-acre Stony Man Mountain Tract. Copper had not been mined there since before the Civil War.

After being shown around the mountain area by a Shenandoah Valley resident, Pollock returned to his father in Washington, D.C. with tales of a high mountain retreat where a resort could be developed "cool, up among the clouds, sparkling springs, glorious sunsets, majestic views, and only ninety miles from Washington." The senior Pollock soon visited the mountain with other investors. Seeing the quality of the land, the group agreed to back the younger Pollock's dream of a resort on Stony Man Mountain. He led the first camping party in 1888 and sold the first cabin lots in 1889. Through lawsuits, paying off debts, burning of the existing buildings, and the death of his father and another partner in 1893, Pollock gained control of the property and reopened his Stony Man Camp in 1894.

Thus began the decades long infatuation with the Blue Ridge Mountains of George F. Pollock, or "Polly" as he was known to his friends. Dashing and dauntless, Pollock dressed in hunting shirt and trousers, boots, ten-gallon hat, a .45 revolver strapped to his hip, and bugle in hand that he blew at every opportunity. In such garb, he lavishly entertained his guests.

Most guests in 1894 stayed in tents furnished with cots, chairs, and washstands, and Pollock advertised "large camp-fires every pleasant night" and "tramping parties . . . every pleasant day." The tents were eventually replaced by wood-frame cottages, shingled in chestnut tree bark or covered in chestnut siding. A recreation hall and a dining hall were constructed. Guests enjoyed picnics, swimming at the head of Whiteoak Canyon, musical shows, and elaborate pageants.

In the forty years that Pollock operated "Skyland," as the Stony Man Camp came to be known, he did much to preserve the mountain region, putting out forest fires and working to prevent logging. Pollock's wife, Addie Nairn, whom he married late in life, purchased the stand of great hemlock trees in the area that came to be called "The Limberlost." So when Secretary of Interior Hubert Work established the Southern Appalachian National Park Committee in 1924 to recommend a location for a national park in the southern Appalachians, Pollock with Harold Allen and George H. Judd made an official request that the Blue Ridge be considered for the site of the national park. Ferdinand Zerkel joined in promoting the Blue Ridge location.

These supporters of a national park in the Blue Ridge soon formed the Northern Virginia Park Association with Pollock as president. They convinced members of the National Park Committee to visit the Blue Ridge, and Pollock hosted the members at Skyland and guided them through the mountains. By the end of 1924, the Committee recommended national parks for both the Blue Ridge and the Great Smoky Mountains to the south. For the Blue Ridge park, Harlan P. Kelsey, a member of the Committee, suggested "Shenandoah," the name of the river and valley to the west.

In 1925, President Calvin Coolidge signed a bill establishing procedures for carving out the two parks. Virginia governor, Harry F. Byrd, Sr., who was one of the earliest lot owners at Skyland and supported the formation of a national park, initiated the state's effort to raise funds for purchase of the land. The bill to establish both the Smokies park and Shenandoah National Park was passed by Congress and signed by President Coolidge on May 22, 1926; the initial proposal for Shenandoah was a minimum of 521,000 acres.

Fund raising by the state was conducted by the Conservation and Development Commission, headed by William E. Carson, an enthusiastic supporter. A new Shenandoah National Park Association assisted with the effort. Although fund raising continued for a few years, there seemed no hope of getting enough money to purchase the required acreage. And so the minimum was twice reduced, the last time to 160,000 acres.

In 1927, the Potomac Appalachian Trail Club formed to promote the route of the Appalachian Trail through the Blue Ridge and to support the establishment of a park. PATC members built many of the trails now on park land.

Harold Allen, one of the early supporters, revived the suggestion of a scenic highway along the spine of the Blue Ridge that had been proposed as early as 1914. The suggestion was included in the final report of the Southern Appalachian National Park Committee as a "skyline drive." In 1930, President Herbert Hoover, who the year before had established his summer White House on the Rapidan River within the proposed boundaries, asked that plans be prepared for a Skyline Drive. Work began in 1931.

In 1933, the Civilian Conservation Corps came to fight fires and help develop roads and facilities; there were eventually six CCC camps in the area. In 1934 the central portion of Skyline Drive opened to the public. In 1935, Virginia donated 176,429 acres for the park. President Franklin D. Roosevelt dedicated Shenandoah National Park at Big Meadows on July 3, 1936. A few months later, the northern section of Skyline Drive opened.

During the years the park took shape, the mountain people who lived within the boundaries were bought out; some had to be evicted. Most of the mountain homes of these people were torn down. Pollock who had sold his land for the national park, continued to operate the Skyland resort as a concession. In 1937, he sold his business interests in Skyland to the Virginia Sky-Line Company, Inc. Pollock and his wife kept a life-time lease on their Skyland cottage, Massanutten Lodge, which along with other of the old cottages, still stands among the more modern buildings and cabins that make up the Skyland resort of today.

Other service facilities were constructed at Dickey Ridge, Lewis Mountain, Big Meadows, and Elkwallow by the new concessionaire during 1938-39. In 1939, the southern section of Skyline Drive opened. In 1950 the Shenandoah Natural History Association was established to promote education and interpretation. The Dickey Ridge Visitor Center opened in 1958, and the Harry F. Byrd Sr. Visitor Center, in 1966. In 1972 ARA Services took over the concessions operation, including Skyland, and is known today as ARAMARK Virginia Sky-Line Company.

In 1976, 79,579 acres of the park was designated wilderness through legislation authored by Senator Harry F. Byrd, Jr. Today, the park encompasses 196,466 acres. Nearly all the park facilities and Skyline Drive itself have been determined to be eligible for the National Register of Historic Places.

Massanutten Lodge

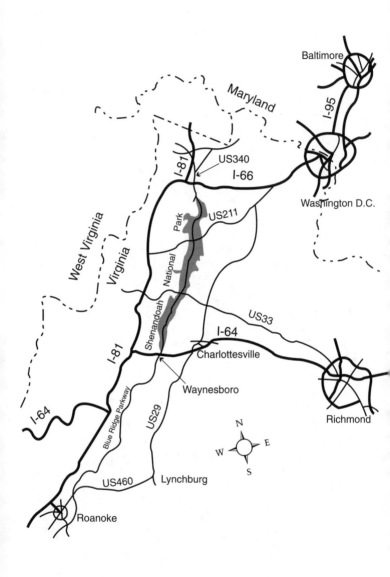

Map 1. Getting to Shenandoah National Park

Getting There

Shenandoah National Park lies 70 miles west of Washington, D.C. in northwest Virginia. This long, narrow park stretches along the crest of the Blue Ridge Mountains for about 75 miles. It's bisected by the 105.4-mile Skyline Drive, which for the most part follows the Blue Ridge crest, with a marker post at each mile numbered north to south. The Drive is the primary access for the park, offering not only scenic overlooks, but also access for most of the trails in the park.

Front Royal lies at the northern end of Skyline Drive just south of I-66. So from Washington, D.C., take I-66 west and at Exit 6 turn south on US340 to pass through Front Royal and pickup Skyline Drive at the northern end of the park. From the west, take I-66 east to Front Royal from I-81, the major north-south route that parallels the national park. If you are coming from the south, you may want to enter the park at its southern end at Waynesboro on I-64, taking that interstate east from I-81 or west from Charlottesville and Richmond.

Highways that pass through major gaps in the Blue Ridge divide the national park into three districts. US211, which runs from I-81 on the west to US29/15 to I-66 on the east passes through Thornton Gap in the park. The entrance there is 80 miles from Washington, D.C. The North District lies between Front Royal on the north and Thornton Gap on the south.

US33, from I-81 on the west to US29 on the east, passes through Swift Run Gap. The park's Central District lies between Thornton Gap on the north and Swift Run Gap on the south. The South District lies between Swift Run Gap on the north and Waynesboro on the south at Rockfish Gap. US29 parallels the park on the east from Charlottesville north to I-66.

Small airports are located at Charlottesville on the east and Grottoes on the west. Washington, D.C. has the nearest major airports.

For access to Skyline Drive, you must stop at one of the four entrance stations--Front Royal, Thornton Gap, Swift Run Gap, or Rockfish Gap--and purchase either a seven-day or an annual pass.

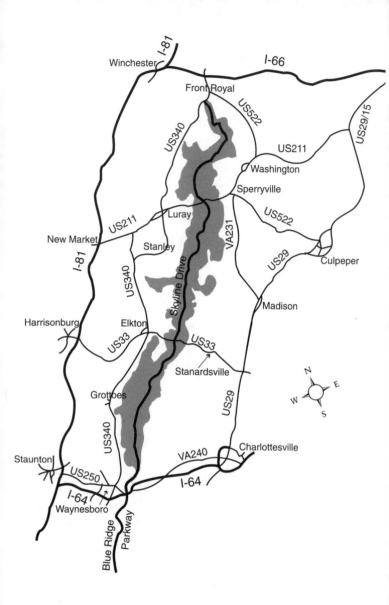

Map 2. Access to Shenandoah National Park

Geology

The Blue Ridge Mountains of Virginia are part of the narrow Blue Ridge Province that stretches from New England south into Tennessee and North Carolina, part of the Appalachian region. Sandwiched between the foothills of the Piedmont to the east and the Valley and Ridge Province to the west, the Blue Ridge forms a prominent mountain range rising three thousand feet above the surrounding terrain. The tallest mountains are Hawksbill at 4050 feet and Stony Man at 4011 feet.

The core rock of the Blue Ridge formed during the early Precambrian period. Deep in the earth, granite, now known as Old Rag Granite, and granodiorite, a quartz rock known as the Pedlar Formation, crystallized out of molten rock. In the late Precambrian, more molten rock pushed its way up through fissures so that lava and volcanic ash spread in a thick layer known as the Catoctin Formation over most of what would be the Blue Ridge Mountains. The Catoctin lava covered and intermingled with sediment from highlands to the west, the heat and mineralizing liquids and gases of the lava solidifying the sedimentary material into a layer known as the Swift Run Formation. This mixture of the Catoctin and Swift Run produced rock of three types: greenstones formed from basaltic lavas, purple slate formed from layers of volcanic ash, and sedimentary rock from solidification of sands, clays, and stones.

With the end of volcanism, streams flowed across the lava plains, depositing mud, sand, and quartz stones that later solidified into the Weverton Formation. The land, which began subsiding during the period of volcanism, continued a downwarping, so that bogs and lagoons formed as the eastern sea invaded during the Cambrian period, about 600 million years ago. The sea deposited muddy sands and clays that became the Hampton Formation. Advancing seas left beach sands that later solidified into quartzites of the Erwin Formation.

The Cambrian period was followed by three periods of mountain building due to the tectonic forces of continental plate movement. The earliest uplift occurred during the Ordovician Period in mountain building now known as the Taconic orogeny, beginning about 500 million years ago. The uplift was caused by the convergence of an island arc with what would be the North American continent. By the end of the Silurian period, 400 million years ago, the Taconic Mountains had been worn down by erosion.

Then in the Devonian Period new mountains arose in the Acadian orogeny as a result of the collision of the North American plate with northern Europe, or perhaps South America. Although erosion began to wear down these new mountains, they were not completely eroded before the collision of North America with the African continental plate produced the Alleghenian orogeny, resulting in much folding and warping and additional uplift 300-250 million years ago. Over the next 100 million years, erosion nearly leveled this range of mountains.

The Appalachian Mountains of today, including the Blue Ridge, are the result of secondary uplift called "isostatic adjustment." In the process, uplift occurs as the weight of overlying layers is removed by erosion and less dense rock below is forced upward by surrounding dense rock. As the ancient mountain range eroded down, reducing the weight above, less dense rock below pushed upward in several intervals of uplift, creating the Blue Ridge anticline, in which stratified layers bent upward. Erosion occurred continuously. Eventually, rock from deep in the earth was uplifted, and erosion exposed the Old Rag Granite and the Pedlar Formation that had formed a billion years ago in the Precambrian.

Now, Old Rag granite and Pedlar granodiorite are exposed on occasional peaks in Shenandoah National Park. Catoctin greenstone lavas top most of the high ridges with interlayered Swift Run. The Weverton, Hampton, and Erwin Formations are exposed along the slopes of the mountains, in the hollows and creek runs. In the central and south sections of the park, magma intruded the Blue Ridge during the Triassic period, leaving vertical dikes of dense greenish crystalline rock.

As you explore the trails of Shenandoah, you'll become familiar with these rock types: granite on Old Rag Mountain, Catoctin greenstone along the high ridges, sedimentary rock in the creeks hollows.

Human History

When John Lederer, a German explorer, came to the Blue Ridge in 1669, he met the Monacan and Manahoac peoples and found them peaceful and intelligent, with a symbolic language and a rudimentary calendar. By 1750 the Indians were mostly gone. Many had died of white men's diseases; others were forced off their lands; the remainder were absorbed by other native groups, especially the Iroquois that came to dominate the region.

Other white men had surely penetrated the region earlier than Lederer. But he was the first to leave a written record and so is credited as the first known white man to climb the Blue Ridge in the region of the Shenandoah, an Indian word that likely means "daughter of the stars." Whether the Indians were taken with the reflection of stars on the waters of the river to the west that now bears the name "Shenandoah," or they were awed by the upward sweep of mountains that seemed to touch the star-studded night, either seems appropriate.

Fur traders and other explorers followed Lederer into the Blue Ridge. Although a few explorers settled in the wilderness, some with Indian wives, British hold on the region remained tentative. When Alexander Spotswood assumed governorship of the Virginia colony in 1710, he feared the French might push down from the north to claim lands to the west. To check such a movement, he wanted to extend English settlement to the mountains and over the Blue Ridge.

Spotswood encouraged settlement by establishing a fort and trading post near the Blue Ridge and inviting people to settle on land he acquired. Then to open up the mountains themselves, he led an expedition in 1716 to cross the Blue Ridge. Traditionally it's said Spottswood's group of 50 gentlemen, rangers, Indians, and servants crossed the mountains at Swift Run Gap, but he may well have crossed elsewhere, probably Milam Gap. The men descended the west side of the mountains and arrived at the South Fork of the Shenandoah River before turning back. Afterward, Spottswood gave each of his gentlemen explorers a small golden horseshoe and dubbed them the "Knights of the Horseshoe," since the horses had to be shod for the rough mountain journey.

While Spotswood encouraged settlement in the southern Blue Ridge, another Englishman laid claim to the northern mountains. In 1649, King Charles II bestowed on seven English noblemen a region called the "Northern Neck," delineated by the Chesapeake Bay, the Potomac River, the Rappahannock River, and a straight line connecting the headwaters of the two rivers. One of the nobles, Lord Culpeper, gained control of the entire Northern Neck, and when he died, the land passed down through his wife and daughter to his grandson, Thomas, the sixth Lord Fairfax.

When Lord Fairfax first visited his property in 1736, he was so enamored of the place that he returned in 1747 to live. Even before his return, Fairfax and the Virginia Colony were disputing the southwestern boundary of the Northern Neck, that straight line running from the source of the Rappahannock to the source of the Potomac. A survey was conducted in 1746 to determine the Fairfax Line. The surveyors chose the headwaters of the Conway River as the source of the Rappahannock, and so surveyed a line from there through Bootens Gap in the Blue Ridge to the Potomac, incorporating 5,280,000 acres in the Fairfax lands. Even so, the line remained in question and land ownership in this central portion of the Blue Ridge continued to be disputed into the next century, especially with James Barbour, who had purchased much of the southern Blue Ridge in 1730.

Lord Fairfax to the north and Barbour to the south sold and leased Blue Ridge land over time so that the lands were gradually carved into smaller plots as people settled the region. The young George Washington helped survey the Fairfax property.

The lands were first carved into huge plantations. Eventually these were subdivided, becoming smaller farms, but at times still numbering in the thousands of acres. Many of the landowners lived in the valleys to the east and west and used the mountain pastures as summer grazing lands for their livestock. Germans that settled in the surrounding valleys constituted a large percentage of the landowners. English and Scotch-Irish constituted most of the remainder, many of whom settled the mountains, living in homes that ranged from clapboard houses to ramshackle cabins. As elsewhere when wilderness was settled, some settlers were squatters who had no claim to the land. Others lived with permission on land owned by valley residents in exchange for watching over the landowner's livestock and buildings.

Trails and wagon roads crossed the mountains so valley farmers on the west could trade with populations in the east. Many routes were taken over by individuals and companies who maintained the roadbeds and turned the routes into toll roads. The roads crossed gaps in the mountain ridge, such as Thornton, Swift Run, and Rockfish Gaps that are still in use. During the Civil War, armies rode through the gaps from battles in the Shenandoah Valley to struggles in the east.

The mountain people cleared the lands for pastures and gardens, using the trees for construction and fuel. They hunted wild animals and gathered nuts, berries, and other forest edibles. They traded what they grew and gathered for items they could not produce themselves, such as sugar and coffee. Legal liquor production, and after Prohibition, illegal, was a means for having a cash income. In later years, many mountain people sold their produce to George Pollock's Skyland resort.

Cutting the mountain forests became an industry in which mostly portable sawmills produced lumber and railroad ties. Tanneries in the valley needed tanbark, which the local people stripped from chestnut oak trees and hauled off the mountains; the bark was a source of tannin for making leather from hides.

In the western foothills, mining operations pulled iron ore from the earth and used the forests to produce charcoal that fueled the smelting furnaces. Manganese was also mined that when combined with iron produced a tough, malleable steel. Copper mines operated on Stony Man Mountain and in Dark Hollow.

In 1934, 465 families representing 2276 people lived within the proposed park boundaries. Only 197 of these families owned the land they lived on; people outside the park owned 93% of park lands. During the years the park was established, the numbers fluctuated with people leaving on their own and others entering the park area. Eventually, the federal government relocated 172 families in new homestead communities surrounding the park, and the state with federal aid took care of 71 families.

A few elderly folk with their families were allowed to live out their lives at their homes in the park. In 1940, 19 families totaling 78 people still lived in the park. The last died in 1979.

Plants and Animals

At one time or another, large sections of the forests of Shenandoah National Park were cut for lumber and fuel and tanbark, or just to clear the land for crops and pasture. But small stands of big trees can still be found along some streams in the park, and a few larger patches remain, the most notable being the virgin hemlock forest saved by Addie Pollock.

With the park lands preserved and protected for the last sixty years, the forests have returned. And so you'll find today a rich, dense forest supporting a treasure of wildlife.

A segregation of forest communities occurs because of differences in elevation, exposure, and moisture. Chestnut oak forests with associated red oaks, hickories, and pines dominate the exposed ridges and south-facing slopes that are more sunny and dry. The understory consists of dogwood, mountain laurel, and striped maple.

Farther down the mountain slopes stand the red oak forests, with white oaks, white ash, and red maple associated. Red oaks are probably the most abundant trees in the park.

The more moist coves support cove hardwood forests dominated by red oak, ash, yellow poplar, and basswood. The understory contains spicebush, hophornbeam, and striped maple.

Yellow poplar forests occur below the cove hardwood forests where streams broaden and the land is even more moist. Among the associated trees are oaks, white ash, white pines, alder, sycamore, and birch. The understory consists of spicebush, maples, and dogwood.

These four are the dominant forests of the park. However, smaller patches of other forests occur. Black locust and oak-pine forests have appeared on lands that were cleared or burned over; they will eventually be replaced by other forest types. Small hemlock forests can be found along streams. Isolated northern hardwood forests of birch, red oak, and basswood stand on high, rocky, north-facing slopes.

From a distance, a haze can be seen over the mountain forests that is natural in origin but is today augmented by air pollutants. The trees of the forests expel hydrocarbon molecules of isoprene

14

and more complex terpenes. The molecules break down and recombine to form molecules large enough to refract sunlight and lend a blue color to the haze. And so, the mountains have been called the "Blue Ridge."

The forests support a multitude of wildlife. The most prominent is white-tailed deer. The animal was hunted for its meat, and habitat was lost as lands were cleared; so when the park was established, the deer were gone. A few were reintroduced to park lands in 1934, and the numbers have since expanded to several thousand. They can be found along Skyline Drive, grazing on the grass that grows in the open and darting across the road, fearless where hunting is no longer allowed.

Several hundred black bear inhabit the park, subsisting primarily on nuts, berries, acorns, fruits, insects, and roots. Fewer in number and more shy than deer, bears are more difficult to see. But in a week of visiting the park and hiking or riding the trails, you'll likely spot one.

In addition to deer and bear, the park contains another 48 species of mammals, including the familiar squirrel, rabbit, skunk, opossum and the less familiar bobcat, grey fox, raccoon.

The park streams support 20 fish species. Amphibians and reptiles of 60 species lurk on the forest floor. The forest contains about 20,000 insect species. Birds of 200 types either live in the park or pass through with the seasons.

Unfortunately, the forests of the Blue Ridge are undergoing change. The gypsy moth was first noticed in the park in 1983; the caterpillars of the moth eat the leaves of oak trees. With repeated defoliation, the oaks become susceptible to diseases and other insects and eventually die. Over 100,000 acres of the park are affected, although at this writing the moths are at a low level. The hemlock woolly adelgid, another exotic pest, sucks sap from the base of hemlock needles, causing defoliation and eventual death of the tree; nearly all park hemlocks are infested.

With these attacks and the effects from pollutants and other insects, the Blue Ridge forest will change over time. Less susceptible species may come to dominate where the oaks and hemlocks once stood, just as other trees replaced the chestnut tree that was virtually eradicated by a blight in the 1920s and '30s. The forest will change, but it will endure.

NEIGHBOR MT. TR.
SKYLINE DRIVE 0.5
HULL SCHOOL TR. 0.5
APPALACHIAN TR. 0.6

Trail junction post

Out There

Nearly five hundred miles of trails wander through Shenandoah National Park. Hiking trails are marked with a blue blaze. The Appalachian Trail has a white blaze. Horse trails, which may also be used by hikers, have a yellow blaze. A double blaze on these pathways indicates a turn in the trail or an intersection.

You may ride bicycles on Skyline Drive and on public roads in developed areas. Bicycles are not allowed on trails or fire roads, other than the paved path through the Big Meadows complex and the first mile of the Rapidan Fire Road.

At virtually every trail junction you'll find a concrete post with metal bands imprinted with trail information. So if you have a trail map and read the information at each junction, you should be able to find your way around. Still, pay attention to where you are going so you can at least retrace your steps to get back out if you lose your way. We expect you to assume full responsibility for knowing where you are going and for not getting lost.

Always let someone know where you are going. If you get lost, do not leave the trail; search parties will always look for you on the trail first.

Trail Descriptions

Skyline Drive travels 105.4 miles through the center of the park, following the main Blue Ridge. Each mile is marked by a concrete post on the west side of the Drive, with mileages running north to south.

Because Skyline Drive is the main access to trailheads in the national park, we begin our trail descriptions at the north entrance at Front Royal and work our way south, ending at Rockfish Gap. As part of our trail information, we include a description of Skyline Drive that tells what you'll encounter as you drive from one trailhead south to the next.

In the directions, we often refer to the "west" or the "east" side of the Drive. Because of the winding nature of the road, you may in fact be facing south or north. "West" refers to the right side of the Drive, and "east" refers to the left side of the Drive while driving north to south.

The accompanying maps are designed to help you find the access points and trailheads. The trail numbers correspond to the numbers on the maps.

For each trail description, we give the distance, indicating "one-way" whenever the trail is not a loop. For those who prefer short outings, we often give the distance to an attraction part way that can be your destination.

We also give a rating of easy, moderate, or difficult. This rating is our subjective judgment of the strenuousness of the trail. While a 10-mile trail would be difficult for anyone not used to hiking, it might be rated easy if it has fairly easy walking. So look not only at the degree of difficulty, but also at the distance and the elevation change.

The elevation gain or loss we give for a trail indicates a difference in elevation between the trail's highest and lowest points. But there could be several ups and downs along the way. We use "elevation change" for the difference between the lowest and highest points on a loop trail, because if you are covering a loop, you will gain and lose the same elevation. We also use "elevation change" when the hike is one-way but the highest or lowest point is along the trail.

We also list cautions, or warnings, about what you might encounter on the trail, such as creek crossings, rocky footing, steep climbs and descents.

Trail connections are included so you may combine several trails for longer outings. To help in making these trail connections, we also include a trail index.

Then, after briefly mentioning the trail's attractions and giving directions to the trailhead, we describe what you'll encounter along the trail. The mileages given in the descriptions are almost always cumulative. If you want to hike or ride the trail in the reverse direction from our description, it will probably be helpful if you calculate the reverse mileages.

Preparations

Even if you are out for only a short time, you should wear walking shoes or hiking boots. Carry along water, a lunch or snacks, rain gear, a first aid kit, and a map and compass; and just in case you get lost or injured, bring along extra clothes, a knife, a flash-light, a lighter or waterproof matches plus some firestarter, and a plastic sheet or emergency blanket.

If you are camping in the backcountry, you'll need everything for surviving in the open overnight and for however many days you choose to be out. If you are inexperienced, the park rangers or your local outfitters can give advice on the equipment needed.

You'll need to check the topographical maps that cover your area. Our maps are designed to help you with the general route and trail connections; they do not provide for detailed navigating. At the minimum, you should have along a trail map that gives you an overall view of the park and the trail connections; you are given a map of the park when you enter and pay your entrance fee. A much more detailed map for each section of the park is available from the Potomac Appalachian Trail Club, and a detailed map of the entire park is available from Trails Illustrated. You'll find these for sale at the park headquarters and visitor centers and from the Shenandoah Natural History Association. You may also order these maps from Mountain Laurel Place; see the order form in the back of this book.

Precautions

Be especially careful climbing on rocks, hiking or riding along the edge of bluffs, and crossing streams. Do not climb on waterfalls. We expect you to take responsibility for your own safety, keeping in mind that being in a wilderness or backcountry setting far from medical attention is an inherently hazardous activity. It is best to travel with someone; if one of you is hurt, the other can care for the injured and go for help.

Severe weather can alter the terrain. A flood in 1995 and a storm in 1996 felled trees, washed out sections of trail, and as a result, changed the park. We try to note sections of trail that have been affected, which may or may not be repaired or cleared when you get there. Call the park or stop at a visitor center for current information on the trails.

Many trees in the park have died in the past few years from insect infestation, disease, and cold winters. Be on the watch for falling trees and limbs, and do not set up camp under a dead tree.

The northern copperhead and the timber rattlesnake live

here; always watch where you put your feet and hands, and give snakes a wide berth. On warm spring and summer days, gnats, black flies, and mosquitoes might be a bother, so carry along insect repellent. Before starting off on a hike, spray your shoe-tops, socks, and pants with repellent to discourage ticks; one type, the deer tick, can transmit a spirochete that causes Lyme disease. And remember to check yourself after a hike.

Stream crossings can be easy or difficult. After a heavy rain, a stream can be swollen with rushing water. Do not attempt to cross such a stream unless you are sure you can make it. If you cannot see the bottom, you should probably not try to ford.

The weather at Shenandoah is unpredictable, and it can be much colder than expected in spring and fall. In cold and wet weather, you face the danger of hypothermia. The symptoms are uncontrolled shivering, slurred speech, memory lapse, stumbling, fumbling hands, and drowsiness. If you are wet and cold, get under some shelter, change into dry clothes, and drink warm fluids. Get in a sleeping bag, if available. To prevent hypothermia, stay dry, eat even if you are not hungry, and drink water even when you are not thirsty.

Boil all water in the backcountry at least one minute before drinking to destroy bacteria and other microorganisms, including Giardia, a flagellate protozoan causing an intestinal disorder called "Giardiasis." Filters and water purifying tablets can be used, but ask for ones that specifically remove Giardia.

While you're out there, do not disturb cultural sites and do not collect items found in the wilderness. Removal of artifacts prevents accurate archeological surveys in the future.

Camping

There are four campgrounds in the national park: Mathews Arm in the North District, Big Meadows and Lewis Mountain in the Central District, and Loft Mountain in the South District. At this writing, Mathews Arm Campground is closed due to a lack of operating funds. You can make reservations for the Big Meadows Campground by calling 1-800-365-CAMP; the others are first-come, first-served. The campgrounds are closed during the winter; check with the park for the dates of operation.

If you're a long-distance hiker on the Appalachian Trail

(three or more nights in the park), you can stop overnight at seven huts strung along the AT through the park--Gravel Springs and Pass Mountain in the North District, Rock Spring and Bearfence in the Central District, and Hightop, Pinefield, and Blackrock in the South District--and one outside the park where the AT is outside the boundaries at the southern end--Calf Mountain.

You may camp anywhere in the backcountry out of sight of roads and other campers and 30 yards from trails and streams. You must obtain a free backcountry permit, available at the entrance stations, the Dickey Ridge and Big Meadows Visitor Centers, the Loft Mountain and Panorama Information Stations, self-registration stations, or the park headquarters, which is located on the west side of the park on US211.

Bury your waste at least six inches deep and at least 100 feet away from trails, water sources, and campsites. Pack out all trash and litter. Campfires are not allowed.

Bears

Black bears inhabit the national park. These animals are not extremely dangerous; even so, you should take precautions to not attract or irritate the bears.

A mother bear is very protective of her cubs. If you encounter a mother with cubs, or a cub alone whose mother is surely nearby, back off. Do not advance on the bears and do not place yourself between the mother and her cubs. Often while hiking, we see a cub climbing a tree; we do not wait around to see if the cub is just having fun or if its mother has scooted it up the tree thinking we are a danger. We quickly move on.

If you face a lone bear, observe from a distance; back off, if you must, to avoid an encounter, or put a tree between you and the bear. Walking a trail while huddled in our dripping rain gear, we at first did not notice a bear at about thirty yards, which moved off the trail to let us by. If we had seen it first, we would have moved off the trail. After we passed, the bear came back to the trail, and we both went on our way.

Under no circumstances should you feed a bear or leave food for a bear, which could become conditioned to humans, losing its natural fear, and so pose a threat to hikers that come after you.

In the backcountry overnight, all food and trash must be

Black Bear

hung from a tree to keep it away from bears. Use a long rope over limbs from two trees to suspend your pack a minimum of ten feet from the ground and four feet from any tree or limb. Also to avoid encounters, keep cooking and sleeping areas separate. Keep your tent and sleeping bags free of food odors by not putting food in them. If your pack is free of food odors, you may hang only your food and trash bags and keep your pack inside the tent with you; also keep your boots in the tent when you retire.

Appalachian Trail

For 2100 miles the Appalachian Trail travels from Mt. Katahdin, Maine, to Springer Mountain, Georgia. The "AT," as it is commonly referred to, is the longest completed trail in the country and one of the longest in the world. It was the first national scenic trail designated in the United States.

For 94.5 of those many miles, the AT passes through Shenandoah National Park, for the most part following the crest of the Blue Ridge. The trail enters the park below Compton Gap at the northern end of the park and travels the mountain ridge south, crisscrossing Skyline Drive. When the trail leaves the park on the south just beyond Jarman Gap, it still follows Skyline Drive, crossing it twice more and joining it at Rockfish Gap on the southern boundary of the park to cross over I-64.

Because the AT follows the Blue Ridge crest, it offers some of the best views in the park. We do not describe the entire AT in our trail descriptions, but we do take you to some of the more interesting viewpoints, such as Compton Peak, the North and South Marshalls, Hogback and Pass Mountains in the North District; Marys Rock, The Pinnacle, Stony Man, and Bearfence Mountain in the Central District; and Hightop, Big Flat Mountain, and Blackrock in the South District. Along these sections of the AT, you'll often see "through hikers," those headed north to Maine or south to Georgia, or as far as they can walk.

If you intend to hike the AT through the park, you'll need the *Appalachian Trail Guide to Shenandoah National Park* available through the PATC and the Appalachian Trail Conference. You'll find this book for sale at the park headquarters and visitor centers and from the Shenandoah Natural History Association. You may also order the book along with the three district maps from Mountain Laurel Place using the order form in the back of this book.

Picnic Areas and Waysides

You'll find seven picnic areas in the park; each has picnic tables, fireplaces, water fountains, and restrooms: Dickey Ridge (Mile 4.6), Elkwallow (Mile 24.1), Pinnacles (Miles 36.7), Big Meadows (Mile 51), Lewis Mountain (Mile 57.5), South River (Mile 62.8), and Loft Mountain (Mile 79.5).

The concessionaire for the park, ARAMARK Virginia Sky-Line Company, operates three service areas referred to as "waysides"--Elkwallow in the North District (Mile 24.1), Big Meadows in the Central District (Mile 51), and Loft Mountain in the South District (Mile 79.5). Each wayside offers food, gifts, gasoline, restrooms, and telephone. The concessionaire also stocks campstores near the Big Meadows, Lewis Mountain, and Loft Mountain Campgrounds. There's the Panorama Restaurant and Giftshop in Thornton Gap. These facilities are closed in the off-season, contact the park or the concessionaire for the dates of operation.

Horseback Riding

You may ride horses on designated horse trails and some fire roads that are open to horses. For a list of trails and roads open to horses, check the index at the back of this book. Remember that horse trails are also open to hikers.

The park concessionaire operates a stables for guided horseback rides at the Skyland complex. But there is nowhere in the park that privately owned horses can be stabled. You may board a horse at several facilities outside the park; check with the local chambers of commerce or at the park's visitor centers. Horses may then be ridden into the park on trails from the boundaries, or horses may be brought into the park by trailer and unloaded at any parking area that is large enough to easily handle the trailer.

The Stony Man parking area at Mile 41.7 and the RV/Trailer service area that gives access to the Tanners Ridge Horse Trail at Mile 51.2 anchor the north and south ends of the Skyland-Big Meadows Horse Trail and so are frequently used. Trailer space is available at Fishers Gap at Mile 49.4 with access to the Red Gate and Rose River Fire Roads and the Skyland-Big Meadows Horse Trail just down the Rose River Fire Road. Space for trailers at the Rapidan Road Parking Area at Mile 51.3 gives access for riding Rapidan Fire Road; from there you can also cross Skyline Drive to pickup the Tanners Ridge Horse Trail and ride it to the beginning of the Skyland-Big Meadows Horse Trail. Parking for one or two trailers at the South River Overlook at Mile 62.7 gives access to the South River and Dry Run Fire Roads, both good horse trails.

With nowhere to leave horses overnight, horseback riding is essentially a day-use activity in the park. Under current regulations, backcountry camping with horses is not practicable--horses must stay on designated trails, but you are not allowed to camp next to a trail and horses must not be left unattended.

When riding in the park, you must hitch horses to rails or picket lines when taking a break; do not tie horses to trees. No grazing is allowed, and hay must not be brought into the park; hay might introduce exotic grasses.

Lodging

In the Central District, the park contains two lodges, Skyland

and Big Meadows, operated by ARAMARK Virginia Sky-Line Company. Both complexes contain lodge rooms, suites, and cabin rooms. ARAMARK also rents cabins and one tent cabin at Lewis Mountain. The lodges are open generally from April to November. Contact ARAMARK for exact dates and advance reservations (800/999-4714).

The PATC maintains six backcountry cabins: Range View in the North District; Corbin, Rock Spring, Jones Mountain, and Pocosin in the Central District; and Doyles River in the South District. PATC Cabins may be rented by the public; call for reservations (703/242-0315). These cabins offer primitive lodging. Bring all supplies with you, including lighting. Bunks, mattresses, blankets, and cooking and eating utensils are supplied. You'll use a wood stove for heating and cooking. You must gather wood, haul water from a spring, and use a privy.

Outside the park, bed & breakfasts and inns are available. In Front Royal at the northern end of the park, Woodward House on Manor Grade (800/635-7011) offers a sumptuous breakfast and only a short walk to the park.

Heritage House Bed & Breakfast (540/675-3207) in "Little" Washington on the east side provides access to trailheads at the edge of the park. Also on the east, near Syria, stands Graves' Mountain Lodge (540/923-4231), a mountain retreat located on a working farm; lodging includes three bountiful meals a day served homestyle on long tables with other guests.

On the west side of the park, Jordon Hollow Farm in Stanley is a restored colonial horse farm converted to a country inn with fine dining at breakfast and dinner (540/778-2285). In Luray, The Mimslyn, a large brick colonial inn built in 1931 with white columned portico and 110-foot long front porch (800/296-5105), possesses a wide lobby with spiral staircase and a large restaurant. Also in Luray, The Mayne View (540/743-7921), a bed and breakfast located in an 1865 Victorian house of Benton Steben, the discoverer of nearby Luray Caverns, offers homemade delicacies at breakfast and tea time.

Many other inns and B&Bs dot the countryside surrounding the park. Check with the local chambers of commerce for further details.

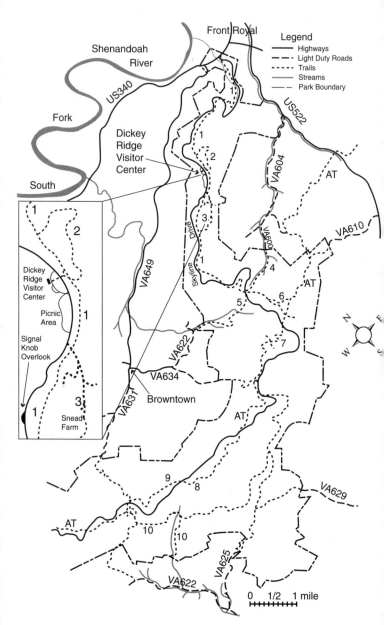

Map 3. Front Royal to Big Devils Stairs

26

⅂ Dickey Ridge Trail

9.5 miles one-way
Moderate
Elevation gain: 1900 ft.
Cautions: Steep ascents
Connections: Fox Hollow Nature Trail, Snead Farm Loop,
Lands Run Gap Road, Hickerson Hollow Trail, Springhouse
Road, Appalachian Trail

Attractions: This northern-most trail climbs Dickey Ridge, following Skyline Drive to Compton Gap where Dickey Ridge joins the Blue Ridge.

Trailhead: The Dickey Ridge Trail begins at the northwest boundary of Shenandoah National Park just south of Front Royal (the name of this town came from an order given by a colonial drill sergeant for his troops to "front the royal oak"). The trail begins at the end of the sidewalk on the east side of US340, which passes through town headed south; you'll reach the end of the sidewalk just after passing under the last traffic light, and there you'll see the beginning of the trail on the left. This works if you're staying nearby in Front Royal, like at Woodward House on Manor Grade where we stayed and walked from the bed & breakfast into the national park. If you need to park somewhere, take US340 south and turn left into the park on the beginning of Skyline Drive. Pass the park entrance sign and in another 100 yards you'll find a pullover area with a sign that indicates you're headed south on the Drive. The Dickey Ridge Trail crosses the Drive here, where you may also begin your hike.

Description: Beginning at Front Royal, bear left off the sidewalk into the woods. In late summer and early fall watch for blooming mistflower, clusters of soft, blue or blue-violet flowers. At 0.1 mile, you'll pass through an open area grownup in grass. When we hiked the trail, a very long black snake took so much time crossing the trail, we finally stepped over it rather than wait any longer; watch out for poisonous snakes though.

The trail leads back into woods but then at 0.2 mile emerges to cross Skyline Drive at the "Southbound" sign. Continue straight, back into the woods which have grown up since the time these were fields before the park was established.

At 0.3 mile, you'll parallel a creek on the right, dry most of the year, that's a tributary of the South Fork of the Shenandoah River. You'll see water in the creek at about 0.5 mile. A side trail to the left at 0.6 mile leads 100 yards up to Skyline Drive where it emerges above the entrance station. After this junction, you'll cross a bridge over the stream you have been following and continue with a slight grade. In late summer, watch for the oval red berries of spicebush, a shrub over three feet tall. We first detected the nice fruity smell of the bush as we walked by; you'll get more of the pleasant odor by rubbing the leaves together.

You'll begin to climb more steeply and then follow a low rock wall that served as a fence on your left beside the trail. At 1.4 miles, the trail switchbacks right and begins a steeper climb, winding up the slope of Dickey Ridge.

You'll emerge on Skyline Drive at 1.9 miles; a white-tailed deer crossed from the other side when we were there; we each passed calmly and went on our way. To make the crossing, you must walk a few yards up the Drive and bear left back into the woods. Still ascending, but not as steeply, you'll pass through a gap in a rock wall at 2.1 miles. Watch for a path right at 2.5 miles that leads out to the Drive across from Shenandoah Valley Overlook.

Continuing up the Dickey Ridge Trail, you'll pass a junction at 4.0 miles with the Fox Hollow Nature Trail to the left and straight ahead at 4.2 miles pass a trail on the right that leads up to the Dickey Ridge Visitor Center across Skyline Drive. Just beyond, you'll pass straight through another junction where the Fox Hollow Nature Trail crosses after having looped through Fox Hollow.

You'll see remains of rock fences on your left and at 4.5 miles pass through a gap in a rock fence. The trail reaches a junction with the Snead Farm Road at 4.8 miles that leads down to the Snead Farm. Turn left on the road and then right back on the Dickey Ridge Trail. The trail then makes a long ascent to pass just below the summit of Dickey Hill at 5.7 miles; you'll then descend to a junction with the other end of the Snead Farm Loop to the left at 6.0 miles. Keep straight to stay on the Dickey Ridge Trail.

The trail descends to cross Skyline Drive in Low Gap at 7.3 miles. You'll then ascend to emerge on the Drive once again at 8.3 miles. There you'll come out to a parking area where the Lands Run Gap Road leads to the right. Cross the Drive and stay right to continue on the Dickey Ridge Trail; you'll also see the Hickerson Hollow Trail to the left.

The trail then ascends Carson Mountain to pass a junction with Springhouse Road at 8.9 miles and connect with the Appalachian Trail at 9.5 miles near Compton Gap. If your goal is to hike the entire length of the park, you'd first hike the Dickey Ridge Trail from the northern park boundary to this junction and then follow the AT south through the park.

Skyline Drive: Headed up Skyline Drive into Shenandoah National Park, you'll pass a road on the left that leads to residences for the Park Service staff and then stop at the Front Royal Entrance Station at Mile 0.6 to pay your entrance fee. At Mile 2.0, you'll pass a parking area on the west side where just up the Drive the Dickey Ridge Trail crosses.

The Shenandoah Valley Overlook lies at Mile 2.8 and offers a view into the Valley and Ridge Province that lies west of the Blue Ridge. In the distance, you'll see Massanutten Mountain that divides Shenandoah Valley, with the South Fork of the Shenandoah River in the valley below and the North Fork of the Shenandoah on the far side of Massanutten; the two forks converge north of Front Royal, which you'll see to your right. Much of Massanutten Mountain is accessible by hiking trails and is part of George Washington National Forest.

2 Fox Hollow Nature Trail Loop

1.2 miles
Easy
Elevation change: 250 ft.
Cautions: None
Connections: Dickey Ridge Trail

Attractions: You'll see the remains of human habitation in the hollow settled by the Fox family.

Trailhead: At Mile 4.6, you'll reach the Dickey Ridge Visitor Center on the west side of Skyline Drive, where you can get maps and information; the building was constructed in 1938 as a dining hall but was converted to the visitor center in 1958. There's now a picnic area to the south. To get to the Fox Hollow Nature Loop, take the path that leads straight out from the visitor center and crosses Skyline Drive to the east side.

Description: From the trailhead sign on the east side of the Drive, turn left to hike the loop clockwise. You'll soon connect with the Dickey Ridge Trail, which cuts across the top of the loop. Turn left on the Dickey Ridge Trail until you reach a junction at 0.2 mile with the Fox Hollow Nature Trail to the right.

Turn right to begin a descent into Fox Hollow, settled by Thomas and Martha Fox in 1837. The Fox descendants lived in the hollow until the state of Virginia purchased the land for the park in 1936. The houses and barns are now gone, but signs of past human habitation remain.

At 0.3 mile, you'll pass the first of several large rock piles left from the clearing of fields, now regrown in trees. The trail passes the rock-walled cemetery at 0.4 mile where Gertrude and Lemuel Fox are buried. Lemuel was the only son of Thomas and Martha to survive the Civil War and so inherited the farm, which later was divided between the four sons of Gertrude and Lemuel.

The trail passes a level area to the left that was the Fox family garden. You'll then reach at 0.5 mile a concrete box protecting a spring that was the first water source for the Dickey Ridge dining hall.

Soon after the springbox, watch for a millstone lying on the ground to the right behind a tree; with no large stream nearby, and so probably no mill, the millstone was most likely brought here for decoration or for use as a stepping stone. The Fox house and barn where located in this area. Just beyond this site, watch for a path left to a rock wall that separated the homesite of Edgar Merchant, the nearest Fox neighbor.

The trail then descends steeply, passing a gathering of golden jewelweed on the left at 0.6 mile. Soon after, watch for a rock-walled depression on the right, and then the trail makes a hairpin turn to the right to follow an old roadbed. On your left, you'll see wire fence topping a row of rock along the roadway. Ascending, the trail curves right at 1.1 miles and reaches a junction with the Dickey Ridge Trail, which to the south leads to the Snead Farm Road in 0.6 mile. Continuing straight, you'll return to the trailhead and cross back over Skyline Drive to return to the visitor center.

③ Snead Farm Loop

2.6 miles
Easy
Elevation change: 500 ft.
Cautions: Steep ascent
Connections: Dickey Ridge Trail

Attractions: The Snead Farm site still includes the old barn.

Trailhead: This loop begins on the Snead Farm Road at Mile 5.1 on the east side of Skyline Drive, just beyond the exit for the Dickey Ridge Picnic Area. After a nice lunch at one of the picnic tables, you can walk to this location by following the road out to the Drive and turn to your right where you'll see the Snead Farm Road on the other side. Or, if you're parked at the Dickey Ridge Visitor Center, you can pick up a paved walkway, at the far end of the lower parking, that leads through the picnic area.

Description: Head down the Snead Farm Road. The Dickey Ridge Trail comes in on the left; it's 0.6 mile to the Fox Hollow Nature Trail if you'd like to walk from there, combining the two trails for a longer outing. Continuing down the Farm Road, you'll see the Dickey Ridge Trail turns off right to continue south.

At 0.1 mile, the road forks, with the right fork leading up to a communications tower on top of Dickey Hill; stay to the left. You'll reach another fork at 0.3 mile where the left fork provides access to the Dickey Ridge water system; take the right fork along the powerline. At 0.5 mile you'll come to a third fork; stay left while the right fork leads up to an instrument tower.

The Snead Farm lies at 0.7 mile. The house is now gone except for the stone foundations, but the overhanging barn still stands. The Carter family originally settled the farm; later the Snead family owned it for a few years before it was acquired for the park.

From the farmsite, the Snead Farm Trail turns to the left at a concrete post. The trail soon curves right along an old roadway. At 0.9 mile, you'll begin a steep ascent; the trail winds right
32

Snead Barn

and left. In late summer, watch for the yellow blooms of false foxglove and the blue and purple of several asters.

At 1.4 miles, you'll reach a junction with the Dickey Ridge Trail. Turn right, passing over Dickey Hill and descending to the Snead Farm Road to complete the loop at 2.6 miles. Turn left to walk back out to Skyline Drive across from the picnic area.

Skyline Drive: Continuing up Skyline Drive, you'll reach a pull-out on the west at Mile 5.3; this overlook has no name but gives a good view of farms in the valley below. This section of valley between the Blue Ridge and Massanutten Mountain to the west is called "Page Valley."

From the Signal Knob Overlook at Mile 5.7, you'll look across the valley to the two ridges of Massanutten, separated by Fort Valley. Germans settled the valley in 1726 and called their community "Massanutten," which is likely a German word consisting of "Masse," meaning "mountain," and "Nute," meaning "groove" or "furrow," referring to the valley in the mountain. The name was eventually applied to the entire mountain ridge, which is topped with a sandstone that resists erosion and protected the mountain as the surrounding valleys were lowered. The small peak at the northern end of Massanutten became "Signal Knob" after the Confederates during the Civil War used it as a signal location.

At Mile 6.8, you'll reach Gooney Run Overlook where to the far right, you'll see part of Dickey Ridge and a meander of the South Fork of the Shenandoah in the valley below. Gooney Run, the creek in Browntown Valley below the overlook, was named for the dog of Lord Fairfax, the Englishman who inherited this region in the early 1700s. At Mile 7.3, you'll look south from Gooney Manor Overlook to see the North and South peaks of Mount Marshall and, farther to the left, Compton Peak. "Manor" refers to a parcel of land; Gooney Manor, which included this area, was one of several parcels that Lord Fairfax retained when he sold most of his land.

You'll pass through Low Gap at Mile 7.9 where the Dickey Ridge Trail crosses; there's a small parking area 100 yards beyond the trail crossing.

4 Hickerson Hollow Trail

1.0 mile one-way
Moderate
Elevation loss: 700 ft.
Cautions: Rocky, moderate descent
Connections: Dickey Ridge Trail, Lands Run Gap Road

Attractions: Hickerson Hollow provides a pleasant walk for hikers and easy access for horses from outside the park.

Trailhead: At Mile 9.2, turn in the parking area at Lands Run Gap on the west side; the Lands Run Gap Road leads from here down the mountain. The Dickey Ridge Trail comes down into the parking area and crosses the Drive to the east side. Walk across the road from the parking area, and you'll see the Dickey Ridge Trail to the right. The Hickerson Hollow Trail begins to the left.

Description: You'll descend from Skyline Drive on an old roadway. Soon, the Hickerson Hollow Trail begins to wind down the mountain, following a tributary of Happy Creek; this stream joins the main creek outside the park in Harmony Hollow. At 0.3 mile, you'll pass through a wet area with trickles of water running across the trail and under the old roadbed in culverts.

At 0.7 mile, a stream on the right crosses under the road to join the main tributary on the left, which with its collection of waters now shows small pools and cascades; the stream is open to catch-and-release fishing only. You'll cross a footbridge over another stream from the right at 0.9 mile; horses must ford. Then at 1.0 mile you'll reach the park boundary where the road is blocked to vehicle access by slabs of rock.

The road continues outside the park as VA600. You can access the trail at this end to the east of Front Royal south of US522 off VA604. Horse riders can enter the park here and after reaching Skyline Drive, turn southeast on the Dickey Ridge Trail or cross the Drive to descend the mountain on the other side down Lands Run Gap Road.

⑤ Lands Run Gap Road

2.0 miles one-way
(Lands Run Falls 0.6 mile one-way)
Easy
Elevation loss: 900 ft.
Cautions: A little rocky
Connections: Dickey Ridge Trail, Hickerson Hollow Trail

Attractions: This old road can be joined with the Hickerson Hollow Trail for a horse ride across the park. It also gives short access to a cascading waterfall.

Trailhead: Begin at the parking on the west side of Skyline Drive at Mile 9.2 in Lands Run Gap. The Dickey Ridge Trail crosses the Drive here, and you can access the Hickerson Hollow Trail on the east side of the Drive.

Description: At the far end of the parking area, you'll find the Lands Run Gap Road descending the mountain. Go around the chain blocking vehicle access and proceed down the road. You'll begin descending more steeply as the road zigzags right and left.

At 0.6 mile the road passes over Lands Run, which flows under the road in a culvert. The stream is open to catch-and-release fishing only. A path to the right leads to the top of Lands Run Falls, a narrow falls where the water jumps from ledge to ledge as it drops steeply into the valley. Take care exploring at the edge; the rocks can be slippery.

The road continues to wind down the mountainside, crossing a tributary of Lands Run and emerging at the park boundary at 2.0 miles. The road joins VA622 outside the park, which can be accessed from VA634 out of Browntown, which is on VA649.

⑥ Fort Windham Rocks/ Indian Run Spring Loop

2.0 miles
Easy
Elevation change: 100 ft.
Cautions: Occasional deadfalls
Connections: Dickey Ridge Trail, Appalachian Trail

Attractions: A pleasant hike through the woods, this loop takes you by rock outcrops and a spring.

Trailhead: On the east side of Skyline Drive at Mile 10.4, you'll find trailhead parking at Compton Gap, the point at which Dickey Ridge joins the main Blue Ridge.

Description: Head up the old road at the far end of the parking area. This is the Appalachian Trail, which crosses Skyline Drive here to continue south.

With a gentle ascent, you'll reach a four-way junction at 0.2 mile on Carson Mountain. To the right, you can descend to Indian Run Spring in 0.2 mile and a PATC maintenance building. Straight ahead, the AT continues north. To the left the Dickey Ridge Trail arrives to end here at the junction with the AT. Turn left on the Dickey Ridge Trail to head to Fort Windham Rocks.

At 0.4 mile, you'll reach the outcrop of Fort Windham Rocks, not spectacular as outcrops go, but a good example of Catoctin lava formations; rocks exposed in the surrounding terrain are Pedlar granodiorite. Continue straight on the Dickey Ridge Trail to a junction at 0.8 mile with the Springhouse Road to the right; the road to the left has been abandoned. The Dickey Ridge Trail continues straight to descend Dickey Ridge to Front Royal in 8.9 miles. The section from here to Lands Run Gap is open to horses to allow access to Lands Run Gap Road and the Hickerson Hollow Trail from Springhouse Road, which is also a horse trail.

Turn right on Springhouse Road. In early fall watch for the red berries of spicebush and, low to the ground, the spike of red berries of jack-in-the-pulpit. The last time we were here, a dead tree fell just after we passed; so take heed of the warnings to watch for falling trees. The road curves right, passes an abandoned road to the left, and reaches a junction at 1.5 miles with the AT.

To the left, the AT heads north 1.1 miles to a junction with the old Compton Gap Fire Road continuing as the Compton Gap Trail, which leads out to VA610 in another half mile. The Compton Gap Trail and this section of the AT is a horse route that ties in with the Springhouse Road. From the junction with the Compton Gap Trail, the AT continues down the mountain to emerge from the park, passing the Tom Floyd camping area, and finally reaching US522 in 5.6 miles.

Where Springhouse Road joins the Appalachian Trail, turn right on the AT to complete this loop. At 1.8 miles you'll return to the four-way junction with Indian Run Spring to the left and the Dickey Ridge Trail to the right. Stay straight to return to the parking area at Compton Gap at 2.0 miles.

7 Compton Mountain

1.2 miles one-way
Moderate
Elevation gain: 500 ft.
Cautions: Rocky
Connections: Appalachian Trail

Attractions: This short hike on the AT takes you to the summit of Compton Mountain where you'll find a couple of overlooks.

Trailhead: At Mile 10.4 the AT crosses Skyline Drive in Compton Gap. From the parking area on the east side, walk across the Drive to your left to pick up the AT on the west side.

Description: Follow the AT up the slope into the woods. In 50 yards, the trail turns left to head south. As you ascend Compton Mountain, you'll pass a large block of stone on the left at 0.2 mile and then the trail swings right. You'll pass another block of stone that presents an example of columnar jointing. The once molten Catoctin lava, when cooled, fractured along crystalline lines, creating polygonal structures of four, five, and six sides. You'll see more of this later on.

At 0.5 mile, the trail swings left in the ascent. You'll pass another block of stone on the left, and then the trail swings right. At 0.8 mile, the AT reaches a four-way junction near the peak of Compton Mountain. The AT continues straight, headed south toward Jenkins Gap. The trails right and left lead to viewpoints.

Take the left trail first. You'll descend to a ledge in 0.1 mile where the trail bears left and drops down the rock. You'll then walk up to a rock outcrop where you can scramble up for a partial view to the south at 0.2 mile. But more interestingly, the rock you're standing on is another example of Catoctin lava columnar jointing. Unfortunately, the columnar structure is not apparent on top because of erosion. To the right of the rock, you can scramble down the steep chute between two blocks of stone to get to the bottom where you'll see the four, five, and six-sided columns protruding from the rock. Only agile hikers should attempt this scramble down to the bottom.

Back at the four-way junction, now take the right path, which takes you over the peak of Compton Mountain at 0.1 mile and then down to a bare rock ledge at 0.2 mile that offers a view to the north. You're facing Dickey Ridge as it ascends to meet the Blue Ridge.

Skyline Drive: From Compton Gap, continue south on Skyline Drive. From Indian Run Overlook at Mile 10.8, you'll have a view north across the valley of Indian Run, which has its beginning at Indian Run Spring, and to the east a view out to the Piedmont. Across the Drive at this overlook stands an exposed wall of Catoctin lava; toward the north end, you'll see more examples of columnar jointing.

At Mile 12.35, the Drive dips through Jenkins Gap; a road on the west leads to a maintenance area. After turning in, you'll see a fire road to the left and just past that is the Jenkins Gap Trail that leads west to cross the AT in 150 yards and then descend the mountain and emerge from the park as VA634 into Browntown. From the Jenkins Gap Overlook at Mile 12.4, you'll have a view east to the Piedmont and Compton Peak to your left. At Mile 12.5, the Mount Marshall Trail follows an old road into the woods, blocked to vehicle access by boulders; the trail provides access to the Bluff Trail in 3.5 miles and the Jordon River Trail in 3.9 miles, which heads east to emerge from the park as VA629. The Mt. Marshall Trail then exits the park to become VA625 at 5.7 miles, which then connects with VA622.

You'll reach Hogwallow Flats Overlook at Mile 13.8 with a wide view to the east of the Piedmont; the name comes from "Piemonte," a foothills region of northwest Italy. At Mile 14.2, the Drive passes through Hogwallow Flats where the AT crosses. Then at Mile 14.9, you'll have a partial view west from the Browntown Valley Overlook; at this writing it's a bit overgrown, but from the north end you can see Dickey Ridge and the community of Browntown in the valley. You'll also see three hills—Round, Long, and Buck Mountains that enclose the valley on the west.

⑧ North Marshall

0.6 mile one-way
Moderate
Elevation gain: 270 ft.
Cautions: Rocky, drop-offs
Connections: Appalachian Trail

Attractions: You'll have grand views from the north summit of Mt. Marshall.

Trailhead: The AT crosses the Drive at Mile 15.95 where there's parking on the east side of the Drive for access to the AT.

Description: The AT passes the back end of the parking area; take the AT to the left, headed north. You'll begin ascending the slope of North Marshall. The trail swings right and then left; through the trees in winter you'll see rock bluffs ahead. At 0.2 mile, the trail switchbacks right in a steeper ascent, and soon after, you'll reach the rock bluff you saw from below where the trail switchbacks left.

You'll ascend to a rock outcrop on the left at 0.3 mile that affords an expansive view west with South Marshall and Hogback Mountain to the left, Browntown Valley below, and Dickey Ridge to the right; Hogback Mountain has the radio towers. The trail turns right at this viewpoint and then soon turns left to continue to ascend the rocky slope of the mountain. At 0.4 mile, you'll reach the ridgeline at another rock outcrop on the left that offers a similar view. The trail levels out along the ridge, passing a couple more outcrops to then make one more ascent to reach the summit of North Marshall at 0.6 mile. The rock outcrops there do not offer a view.

From the summit, the AT descends the rocky slope to eventually cross Skyline Drive in Hogwallow Flats in another 1.5 miles.

View from North Marshall

⑨ South Marshall

0.9 mile one-way
Moderate
Elevation gain: 210 ft.
Cautions: Rocky
Connections: Appalachian Trail

Attractions: Rock outcrops offer additional views to the west.

Trailhead: Access the AT from the parking area on the east side of the Drive at Mile 15.95.

Description: This time, turn right, headed south on the AT. At 0.1 mile, the trail crosses Skyline Drive at an angle to the east side.

You'll ascend gently through the woods, passing mounds of exposed rock. In early spring, when we last hiked the trail, the tops of the bare trees were brushed with a maroon color as new growth pushed its way upward in the warming sun; despite the snow still on the ground and the gray of rock and tree, we knew leaves and flowers would soon color our walks.

The trail levels off at 0.4 mile on the shoulder of South Marshall and then ascends once more to the summit at 0.6 mile. There are no views there; but continue across the summit and begin descending the other side until at 0.7 mile a side path leads right to a rock outcrop and a view west. Continue on down the trail through a snaking curve to a path right and another outcrop at 0.9 mile with a 180-degree view west. Hogback Mountain with its radio towers stands to the left.

The North and South Marshalls were once part of the Manor of Leeds, one of the parcels of land retained by Lord Fairfax. When he died in 1781, his lands were sold to a group of investors, one of whom was John Marshall, who obtained the Manor of Leeds; Marshall served as Chief Justice of the U.S. Supreme Court 1801-1835. Marshall's father, Thomas, had been a surveyor, with George Washington, of Fairfax lands and had given the name "Marshall" to the mountains.

From the overlook, the AT continues across the slope of South Marshall to emerge at Gravel Springs Gap and cross Skyline Drive in another mile.

Skyline Drive: Headed south from Mt. Marshall, you can look back over your left shoulder at Mile 16.1 and see the prominent cliffs of North Marshall; it's an easier view if you're driving north. From the Range View Overlook at Mile 17.1, you'll have a sweeping view of the Blue Ridge range to the south. In the distance, on a clear day, you'll be able to make out the ragged peak of Old Rag Mountain. To the right, look for The Pinnacle and just to its right the outcrop of Mary's Rock; then to the right, you may be able to make out the profile of Stony Man.

10 Big Devils Stairs

3.4 miles one-way
(Big Devils Stairs Overlook 2.4 miles one-way)
Moderate
(Difficult if you return up the creekbed)
Elevation loss: 1400 ft.
Cautions: Steep descent, exposed bluffs
Connections: Browntown Trail, Appalachian Trail,
Bluff Trail, Harris Hollow Trail

Attractions: You'll have a view of one of the deep canyons of the park and, if you're an experienced hiker, an adventure coming back up the creekbed during the dry season.

Trailhead: At Mile 17.6 pull in parking on the east at Gravel Springs Gap. The old road here was once the Browntown-Harris Hollow Road that crossed the mountain. On the west side of Skyline Drive this old road is now the Browntown Trail for horses that descends the mountain to emerge from the park and connect with VA631; the access there is not readily visible. The AT from the north joins this road just west of Skyline Drive and crosses the Drive here to then head south on the east side of Skyline Drive. From the parking area, take the AT into the woods; it parallels the old road on the east as it leads down to the Gravel Springs Hut.

Description: Along the AT in 0.1 mile, you'll reach a junction with the Bluff Trail to the left and the AT continuing straight. Turn left here to descend to a junction at 0.3 mile with the old road you've been paralleling. To the right, you'll see the Gravel Springs Hut, where long-distance hikers may camp; you'll find the spring at your junction with the road. The old Browntown-Harris Hollow Road on down the mountain has become overgrown beyond the hut. Turn left on the road and then turn right to continue on the Bluff Trail.

At 0.4 mile, you'll pass a junction with the Harris Hollow Trail to the left that leads up to the old road and then Skyline

Drive where horses can cross the Drive and take the Browntown Trail down the mountain to the west.

From this left junction, stay straight and curve right as the Harris Hollow Trail and the Bluff Trail coincide. At 0.5 mile, the Bluff Trail turns left while the Harris Hollow Trail continues straight to rejoin the old roadway down the mountain and to emerge from the park on VA622.

Stay left with the Bluff Trail. You'll pass along the slope of South Marshall. The trail passes through rock outcrops and crosses small flows of water. At 1.0 mile, you'll pass through an open area with displays of blue asters in late summer and early fall. The trail drops off to the right and then ascends back to the level at 1.6 miles.

At 1.7 miles, you'll step over a crevice with a stream that is the head of Big Devils Stairs and continue on to a junction with the Big Devils Stairs Trail at 1.8 miles. The Bluff Trail continues on here across the flank of North Marshall to connect with the Mt. Marshall Trail in another 2.1 miles.

Turn right on the Big Devils Stairs Trail. The trail winds down the mountain through stands of laurel out to a bare rock view on the east edge of the canyon at 2.4 miles. We could hear water in the depths of the narrow gorge. Circling ravens gave mournful calls that echoed off the massive rock walls.

The trail skirts the edge of the canyon and then turns away from the edge into the woods to descend the rocky slope steeply by switchbacks to the mouth of the canyon at 3.4 miles. You'll rockhop the stream, which is a tributary of the Rush River; on the other side, the trail continues downstream a few paces to the park boundary and private land, which you may not cross.

From here you must return up the mountain along the Big Devils Stairs Trail, or if it is the dry season and the water in the stream is low, you may follow the streambed back up the canyon. We recommend this alternative route only for experienced hikers and explorers; also, be aware you may run into stinging nettle, a plant that will sting your bare skin. On the day we rockhopped up the creekbed in early Fall, we circled pools and spillways fairly easily. But at two locations, we encountered rock walls that had to be climbed to the levels above in order to continue up the streambed. Eventually we emerged at the head of

46

the canyon to reconnect with the Bluff Trail. You'll then turn left on the Bluff Trail to retrace your steps back to Gravel Springs Gap.

Skyline Drive: From the Gimlet Ridge Overlook at Mile 18.4, you'll see the cliffs of South Marshall to the far right. Far to the left stands Hogback Mountain with Gimlet Ridge running out to the right. Toward the end of the ridge, you'll see the three hills that partially close off Browntown Valley below.

At Mile 18.9 the AT crosses the Drive. You can access this AT crossing from Mount Marshall Overlook on the east side of the Drive at Mile 19.0. From the overlook, you'll see the two Marshalls to the left and to their right the steep slopes of The Peak. Farther to the right, in the valley between the foothills, you'll see the town of Washington, Va., sometimes called "Little Washington." A number of the foothills, including The Peak and Wolf, Jenkins, and Keyser Mountains below, were separated from the main Blue Ridge by erosion along a fault line.

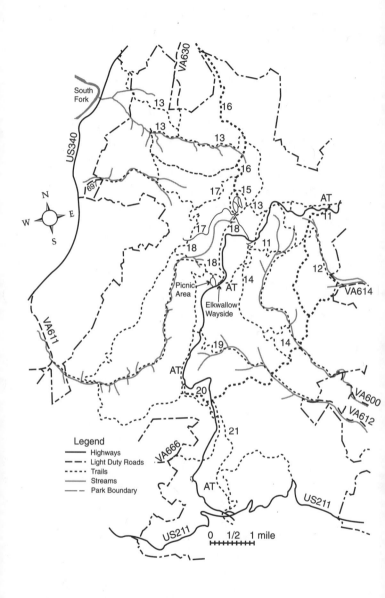

Map 4. Keyser Run to Pass Moutain

48

11 Keyser Run/Pole Bridge Link/Piney Branch/AT Loop

6.8 miles
Moderate
Elevation change: 800 ft.
Cautions: Skyline Drive crossings, steep ascents, creek ford
Connections: Little Devils Stairs Trail, Sugarloaf Trail

Attractions: A quiet walk through backcountry and views along the AT to the west make this a good loop hike.

Trailhead: At Mile 19.4 turn in the Keyser Run Fire Road on the east side where you'll find a paved parking area. On the west side of the Drive, a short connecting trail leads to the AT; this will be the return route. To walk this hike clockwise, head down the Keyser Run Fire Road past the chain gate.

Description: The Keyser Run Fire Road descends gently, crosses a small tributary of Keyser Run at 0.5 mile, and reaches an intersection at 1.0 mile at a point called "Fourway." To the left the Little Devils Stairs Trail descends through a narrow, steep canyon. The Keyser Run Road continues down the mountain to cross the Park Boundary in another 3.3 miles. For this hike, turn right on the Pole Bridge Link Trail just a few paces down the road from the Little Devils Stairs turnoff.

The Pole Bridge Link Trail follows an old roadway through the woods. A couple of small wet-weather streams cross the trail. You'll reach a junction with the Sugarloaf Trail to the right at 1.6 miles. You can make a shorter loop by turning up the Sugarloaf Trail 1.4 miles to the AT and then heading north back to Keyser Run Road for a total of 4.7 miles.

Stay straight to make the longer loop. The Pole Bridge Link Trail descends gently, eventually winding down to a junction at 2.0 miles with the Piney Branch Trail. To the left, the Piney Branch Trail heads down the mountain to the east to follow the Piney River, cross the Hull School Trail, and emerge from the

49

park in 4.4 miles as VA600. Stay straight on the Piney Branch Trail to the west.

Soon two streams that are tributaries of the Piney River cross under the trail in culverts, and at 2.1 miles you must ford the main branch of the Piney River. Here is where a pole bridge once stood, from which the Pole Bridge Link Trail got its name. The bridge washed away some time ago.

From the ford, continue up the old roadway. You'll ascend an eroded, rocky section and then ascend more steeply as the road curves right. At 2.8 miles the trail crosses water from a spring on the left. You'll curve right two more times as the old roadway ascends the ridge to reach a junction with the Appalachian Trail at 3.4 miles. You'll emerge in a clearing where the service road from the Piney River Maintenance Area descends to the Range View Cabin. The AT to the south follows the road to the left for a few paces and then turns off the road to the left to pass near the cabin in 0.4 mile. Turn right to walk the AT to the north on a wide trail.

You'll begin ascending and curve left to walk through boulders and then descend to a crossing of Skyline Drive at 3.8 miles. Just to the right on the Drive, you'll see the Rattlesnake Point Overlook.

Back among trees and boulders, you'll make a steep, winding ascent of Hogback Mountain. At 4.0 miles the trail tops the first of four peaks of Hogback Mountain at a rock outcrop. You'll then descend, swinging left around another mound of rocks, and begin a long steep ascent of the second peak. At 4.4 miles, the trail reaches a junction with the Tuscarora/Overall Run Trail to the left, with the Big Falls of Overall Run 2.8 miles down that trail.

Stay straight on the AT to continue to ascend and top the second peak of Hogback Mountain at 4.5 miles. You'll then descend to pass by AT-access parking and cross Skyline Drive at 4.8 miles. You'll ascend once again to top the third peak of Hogback at 4.9 miles. The trail then descends, passing above the Hogback Overlook on Skyline Drive and swinging right to a junction with the Sugarloaf Trail, which leads 1.4 miles down to the Pole Bridge Link Trail. Stay straight here to swing left up steps and cross Skyline Drive at 5.1 miles.

On the other side of the Drive, walk up the service road that leads to radio towers. Soon the AT turns off to the right; just after the turn, you'll see an old path that leads out to the Drive on the right. But stay straight to ascend steeply, cross the service drive, and reach the fourth summit of Hogback Mountain at 5.3 miles where you'll be among radio towers and small service buildings. Across the summit, you'll begin a descent of Hogback Mountain.

Soon, a path on the left leads to the edge of the mountain and a hang-glider launch area. The day we were there in winter no one was about, unfortunately; we would like to have seen someone launch into empty air from the edge of the mountain. The view is straight down Browntown Valley to Dickey Ridge. Just beyond the launch site, you'll have another view to the left under a powerline that runs to the radio towers on the summit.

Continuing down the AT, you'll reach a junction at 5.4 miles with a side path right that leads down to Skyline Drive in 400 yards. There's a little parking there if you want to make a short trip to the hang-glider launch site. The AT continues straight to cross a couple of knolls and then begin a steep descent. With several switchbacks, you'll drop below the level of Skyline Drive into the gap between Hogback Mountain and Little Hogback. You'll pass below Little Hogback Overlook and ascend to a junction at 6.3 miles with a path right that leads from the overlook to the AT.

Continue ascending to bear left over the low summit of Little Hogback to where the AT turns right at 6.4 miles. At this turn, a path leads left out to a rock outcrop and a good view of Hogback Mountain to your left with Gimlet Ridge running down to Browntown Valley. Continuing on the AT, you'll then descend to a junction at 6.7 miles with the access path right to Keyser Run. Turn right here to cross Skyline Drive at 6.8 miles and close the loop at the Keyser Run Fire Road parking area.

12 Little Devils Stairs/ Keyser Run Loop

5.5 miles
Difficult
Elevation change: 1400 ft.
Cautions: Steep rocky ascent, creek crossings
Connections: Pole Bridge Link Trail, Hull School Trail

Attractions: The ascent through a narrow canyon is one of the most interesting hikes in the park.

Trailhead: You can access this loop hike along the Keyser Run Fire Road from Skyline Drive at Mile 19.4. But we hiked the trail while staying at Heritage House Bed and Breakfast in "Little" Washington, a picturesque hamlet known for its inns and B&Bs and providing access to park trails at the east boundary. On US211/522 south of Washington, turn east on VA622. At 2.0 miles, turn left on VA614, which becomes a graveled road. At 5.2 miles, you'll reach trailhead parking on the right.

Description: The trail enters the woods and drops to cross a small creek and then a larger creek. Bear right past piles of stone from once-cleared fields. At 0.1 mile, curve left up the cove of Keyser Run, the stream flowing from Little Devils Stairs canyon.

Stone walls and piles of stone remain from before there was a national park. You'll drop through a drainage area and ascend to Keyser Run and cross the creek at 0.8 mile. You'll then make a steep, rocky ascent upstream, crossing the shallow creek several times. In spring, petals from tulip poplar blooms litter the path. At 0.9 mile watch for a huge poplar on the right.

The trail continues up the cascading creek, crossing a talus slope and at 1.2 miles entering Little Devils Stairs, a narrow vertical-walled canyon. Keep an eye on the blazes through the rocky gorge. At 1.5 miles, the creek glides down smooth rock; soon after you'll pass through a rock chute just after a cascade.

At 1.7 miles, the trail turns left away from the creek just

Falls in Little Devils Stairs

before a cascading falls. You'll then wind up the slope to reach the Fourway junction with the Keyser Run Fire Road at 2.0 miles. To the right on the fire road, you can reach Skyline Drive in 1.0 mile at Mile 19.4 at the beginning of Keyser Run Road. Just down the road to the left, the Pole Bridge Link Trail heads south to link with the Piney Branch Trail. To complete this loop, stay down the fire road to the left. The road is blazed yellow for horse use.

As you descend the steep road, watch for stands of maiden-hair fern in spring and, in summer, blackberries and raspberries. At 3.8 miles, you'll pass under a powerline and stay straight. On a more level area at 4.1 miles watch for peculiarly twisted sassafras trees. At 4.3 miles you'll pass the walled Bolen Cemetery on the left, with also Dwyers, Tindalls, and Baileys buried there, and reach a junction at 4.4 miles. To the right is the Hull School Trail that leads south to the Piney Branch Trail. Stay left with the Keyser Run Fire Road.

You'll crisscross under the powerline a couple of times as the road descends to the park boundary at 5.3 miles. Go around a chain blocking vehicle access and continue down the road, which follows the park boundary on the left. You'll pass a private road up to the right and return to the trailhead parking at 5.5 miles.

Skyline Drive: From the Little Hogback Overlook at Mile 19.7, you'll have a view down Browntown Valley with Hogback Mountain to your left. The AT can be accessed by a short path at the north end of the overlook parking. North on the AT for 0.1 mile offers a view west from the summit of Little Hogback.

At the Little Devils Stairs Overlook at Mile 20.1, you'll see the gorge of Little Devils Stairs below and "Little" Washington in the distance. At Mile 20.4, a graveled pullout on the west side of the Drive gives you access to the AT in a 400-yard uphill hike to the hang-glider launch site. At Mile 20.8, the AT crosses Skyline Drive; you'll also see the service road on the west side for the radio towers on the summit of Hogback Mountain. Just beyond this AT crossing lies the Hogback Overlook; the ridge running down from Hogback Mountain splits into Mathews Arm to the left and Gimlet Ridge to the right.

⅟⅊ Tuscarora/Overall Run Trail

5.8 miles one-way
(Overall Run Falls [Big Falls] 3.2 miles one-way)
Moderate
Elevation loss: 2600 ft.
Cautions: Rocky, steep descent
Connections: AT, Traces Nature Trail, Mathews Arm Trail,
Thompson Hollow Trail, Beecher-Overall Connecting Trail

Attractions: This hike down the western side of the Blue Ridge passes by the two falls of Overall Run.

Trailhead: At Mile 21.1 turn in a paved parking area on the west side of the Drive where you'll have access to the AT, which crosses the Drive on the south end of the parking area.

Description: Take the AT to the right, headed south. You'll pass over one of the peaks of Hogback Mountain among witch hazel, small trees that bloom in fall with yellow clusters along the stems. At 0.4 mile, you'll reach a junction with the Tuscarora/Overall Run Trail on the right. The AT continues straight to cross Skyline Drive once again in another 0.6 mile.

Turn right on the Tuscarora/Overall Run Trail; this was also called the "Big Blue" Trail, but that named has recently been dropped. The trail winds down to a junction at 1.2 miles. To the left a connector trail leads 0.1 mile over to the Traces Nature Trail that circles the Mathews Arm Campground. Turn right to stay on the Tuscarora/Overall Run Trail.

The trail ascends to then turn left, pass a large boulder, and wind down a steep, rocky slope. You'll bottom out to cross a small stream in a wet area. You'll ascend again and reach a junction with the Mathews Arm Trail at 2.7 miles. This trail is an old road that leads left to the Mathews Arm Campground in 1.4 miles. Stay to the right on the road where the two trails now coincide. At 2.8 miles, the Tuscarora/Overall Run Trail turns off to the left.

You'll descend steeply to turn right along Overall Run. At

55

2.9 miles, a path to the left leads to a view of the 29-foot-high upper falls. Continue to descend on the steep, rocky path that winds down the mountain. At 3.2 miles you'll emerge onto rock outcrops that afford a distant view of the 93-foot-high Overall Run Falls, or "Big Falls," the highest waterfall in the park. You'll also have a view down the valley of Overall Run, which bears the name of the family that owned the area for generations.

The steep trail continues descending the ridge, crossing Overall Run and then crossing back, to a junction with the Thompson Hollow Trail at 5.2 miles. Here the Tuscarora and Overall Run Trails separate. The Tuscarora turns right on the Thompson Hollow Trail, an old road. At 5.9 miles, that trail forks; stay to the left on the Tuscarora Trail while the Thompson Hollow trail continues straight to emerge from the park as VA630. The Tuscarora continues west to cross a tributary of Overall Run, emerge from the park, and connect with US340 at 8.2 miles. The Tuscarora Trail continues west and north for over 200 miles to form a loop with the AT, which it rejoins near Harrisburg, Penn; the name "Tuscarora" comes from an Indian tribe that lived in the area of Pennsylvania.

The Overall Run Trail continues along the cascading Overall Run past the turnoff for the Thompson Hollow and Tuscarora Trails. At 5.8 miles you'll reach a junction with the Beecher-Overall Run Connecting Trail to the left. The Overall Run Trail now ends at this junction because there is no longer access from outside the park. A long loop can be hiked using the Overall Run Trail, turning along the connecting trail, and then walking up the Beecher Ridge Trail to connect with the Mathews Arm Trail. Turning left you would close the loop at the junction with the Tuscarora/Overall Run Trail, a total of 7.5 miles.

Skyline Drive: From Rattlesnake Point Overlook at Mile 21.9 on the east side of the Drive, you'll have a bird's-eye view of Pignut Mountain, straight out from the overlook. The rock exposed on the west side of the Drive is a good example of Catoctin basalt. The AT crosses the Drive just to the south of the overlook; north along the AT it's 0.6 mile to the Tuscarora/Overall Run Trail.

14 Piney Ridge/Hull School/ Fork Mountain Loop

9.7 miles
Moderate
Elevation change: 1500 ft.
Cautions: Stream fords
Connections: Appalachian Trail, Piney Branch Trail, Hull
School Trail

Attractions: This trail follows some old roads in the area and takes you down along Piney River.

Trailhead: At Mile 22.1 turn up a road on the left that leads to the Piney River Maintenance Area. Just before the maintenance area, stop at the visitor parking on the left. This area was once the site of the Redbird CCC Camp.

Description: From the parking area, walk up the road and turn left down a side road toward the Range View Cabin. At 0.1 mile, just before ranger housing, turn right off the paved road onto a gravel road to continue toward the cabin. At 0.2 mile, you'll reach a junction with the Appalachian Trail coming from the left to join the road and also the Piney Branch Trail leading off to the left.

Continue down the road. In a few paces the AT turns off left, but just continue straight down the road. At 0.8 mile, the AT crosses the road; stay on the road. At 0.9 mile, the Piney Ridge Trail begins on the right. From here the road curves down to a meadow where stands the Range View Cabin, built by the PATC in 1930s.

Turn right onto the Piney Ridge Trail. You'll pass through an old apple orchard and descend gently along the ridge. At 2.0 miles, old trees stood like ghosts in the early morning fog as we passed through a stand of white pine. The trail descends an old roadway to a junction with the Fork Mountain Trail at 3.2 miles.

This will be the return route of the loop. Turn left to continue on the Piney Ridge Trail.

The trail begins a steeper descent into the hollow of Piney River. You'll curve right in the descent through a more open area that was once a field or housesite at 3.4 miles; piles of rock stand in the woods. Up from the clearing and down again, you'll descend along an old roadway. A stream flows under rocks to make its way down to join the Piney River below. At 4.2 miles, you'll reach a junction with the Piney Branch Trail. Turn right.

The trail descends along Piney River to a ford of the stream at 4.5 miles. The Hull School Trail comes in from the left to join the Piney Branch Trail at 4.6 miles; to the left the Hull School Trail leads 0.7 mile to the Keyser Run Fire Road.

Staying with the Piney Branch Trail/Hull School Trail to the right, you'll ford the Piney River again at 4.8 miles. On the other side the two trails split with the Piney Branch Trail leading left to continue down along Piney River and emerge from the park to connect with VA600 in another 1.9 miles. Where the trails split, turn right on the Hull School Trail, which ascends an old road. You'll cross a small stream, pass through an old rock wall and a pile of rocks from a cleared field, and ascend to a junction with the Fork Mountain Trail at 5.3 miles. The Hull School Trail continues south down the old road to cross the Thornton River at the site of the old Hull School and emerge on Skyline Drive in another 2.9 miles.

At the junction on Fork Mountain with the summit to the left, turn right off the Hull School Trail onto the Fork Mountain Trail. You'll ascend through a hardwood forest in a steep ascent, eventually reaching a junction with the Piney Ridge Trail to close the loop at 6.5 miles. It's then 3.2 miles back to the Piney River Maintenance Area.

15 Traces Nature Trail Loop

1.7 miles
Moderate
Elevation change: 200 ft.
Cautions: Steep descent
Connections: Elkwallow Trail, Tuscarora/
Overall Run Trail, Mathews Arm Trail

Attractions: This loop circles the Mathews Arm Campground while passing the traces of past human habitation.

Trailhead: At Mile 22.2, pull in the graveled parking on the right, which is beside the entrance to the Mathews Arm Campground. At this writing, the campground is closed due to budgetary problems. If the campground is open when you arrive, drive into the campground to access the trail. If it is closed, you must park here and walk in on the paved road, which will add 0.7 mile both ways to your walk for a total of 3.1 miles.

Description: From the parking area, walk down the paved road into the campground; the road descends steeply to the registration building in 0.7 mile. To the right you'll see a parking area for the amphitheater. On the left side of the road, you'll see a post marking the beginning of the Elkwallow Trail that leads 2.0 miles to the Elkwallow Wayside; the trail begins up an old road but soon turns right on a footpath.

At the far right end of the amphitheater parking area, you'll see the trailhead for the Traces Nature Trail. A metal box there usually holds pamphlet guides to the numbered spots along the trail.

Head into the woods. The trail ascends, frequently curving, but mostly curving left as it circles the campground. The numbered posts mark the sites of old roads, housesites, rock piles from cleared fields, rock fences, and forest plants.

At 0.5 mile, at post #9, a trail to the right leads 0.1 mile up to the Tuscarora/Overall Run Trail. The Traces Nature Trail turns left at this junction. You'll then descend steeply into a cove that

59

was once a homesite with stone fences and a spring. At post #16 at 0.9 mile, you'll pass a fenced exclosure that keeps deer out so park staff can study the effects of browsing.

At 1.1 miles, the trail crosses a road that is the Mathews Arm Trail. To the left you can reach the back end of the campground in 0.1 mile. Continuing straight on the Traces Nature Trail, you'll circle the large rocky knoll at the back end of the campground, eventually passing under a powerline and emerging on the park road at 1.7 miles behind the registration building and across from the amphitheater parking area.

1⑥ Mathews Arm Trail

4.4 miles one-way
Moderate
Elevation change: 1300 ft.
Cautions: Steep descent off ridge
Connections: Traces Nature Trail, Weddlewood Trail,
Beecher Ridge Trail, Tuscarora/Overall Run Trail

Attractions: This old road serves to connect several trails behind the Mathews Arm Campground.

Trailhead: The trail begins at the back of the Mathews Arm Campground. If the campground is still closed; you'll have to park at Mile 22.2 on Skyline Drive and walk in along the paved road for a mile, bearing right, to the very back of the campground to a rocky knoll. You'll see the old road gated to the right. You may also walk the Traces Nature Trail, which circles the campground and crosses the Mathews Arm Trail; see Trail #15 for details.

Description: The road circles left around the rocky knoll and descends to the crossing of the Traces Nature Trail Loop at 0.1 mile. Stay straight up the old road as it runs along the ridge of Mathews Arm. At 0.4 mile, you'll reach a junction with the Weddlewood Trail to the left, which connects with the Heiskell Hollow Trail; you can use those two trails to loop back to the campground in 2.5 miles; see Trail #17.

Continuing up the road, you'll reach a junction with the Beecher Ridge Trail to the left at 0.9 mile that forms a 6.8-mile loop with Heiskell Hollow Trail, and a 7.5-mile loop with Overall Run Trail. Stay straight; the road swings right through the rocky streambed at the head of Overall Run and reaches a junction with the Tuscarora/Overall Run Trail from the right at 1.4 miles. The road bears left; at 1.5 miles the Tuscarora/Overall Run Trail turns left off the road. The Mathews Arm Trail continues out the ridge to eventually bear left in a steep descent to reach the park boundary at 4.4 miles. Access from there to VA630 is poor.

17 Weddlewood/ Heiskell Hollow Trails

2.5 miles one-way
Moderate
Elevation change: 600 ft.
Cautions: None
Connections: Mathews Arm Trail, Knob Mountain Trail

Attractions: This pleasant walk offers connections for trails on the west end of Mathews Arm Campground.

Trailhead: The Weddlewood Trail turns west off the Mathews Arm Trail at 0.4 mile north of the campground; see Trail #16.

Description: Weddlewood descends following an old roadbed. The road swings left and descends more steeply, eventually reaching a junction with the Heiskell Hollow Trail at 1.3 miles. From this junction, the Heiskell Hollow Trail descends to the west, following the East Fork to emerge from the park on VA697 in 3.2 miles; access there is difficult and not recommended. You can make a 6.8-mile loop with the Beecher Ridge Trail, which joins the Heiskell Hollow Trail 1.8 miles down from this junction.

The Weddlewood Trail ends at the junction with the Heiskell Hollow Trail. Continue straight on what is now the Heiskell Hollow Trail leading toward the campground. You'll ascend the rocky roadbed to reach a junction at 2.1 miles with a road that leads from the campground to the wastewater treatment plant. This is also the Knob Mountain Trail, which in several yards to the right turns off this road to head south along Knob Mountain and connect with the Jeremys Run Trail in 7.1 miles.

Turn left on the gravel road, and at 2.5 miles you'll emerge on a paved road that leads straight into the campground.

Skyline Drive: The AT crosses the Drive just before the Elkwallow Wayside at Mile 24.0 where you can get gas and food.

18 Jeremys Run/Knob Mountain/Elkwallow Loop

5.2 miles
Moderate
Elevation change: 700 ft.
Cautions: Creek ford, steep ascent
Connections: Appalachian Trail, Heiskell Hollow Trail

Attractions: This pleasant circuit hike introduces you to several backcountry trails.

Trailhead: After Elkwallow Wayside, turn in the Elkwallow Picnic Area at Mile 24.1; the road is one-way. At the back end of the picnic area lies the trailhead for Jeremys Run and the AT.

Description: Head straight into the woods from the picnic area on the Jeremys Run Trail. In 200 feet you'll connect with the AT. Your return route will be along the AT from the right; turn left as the AT and Jeremys Run Trail coincide.

At 0.2 mile, you'll pass a spring on the left. Descending, you'll reach a junction at 0.3 mile with the AT turning south toward Thornton Gap. Stay straight on Jeremys Run Trail.

The trail curves right in a descent and at 0.5 mile curves left to cross a shallow stream. The stream flows below on your right. At 0.7 mile the trail joins an old roadbed where you'll bear to the left on the roadway. Continuing to descend, you'll see the convergence of two streams below that form Jeremys Run.

At 0.8 mile, you'll descend to a junction with the Knob Mountain Cutoff Trail. Jeremys Run Trail continues straight on the old roadway down the gorge of Jeremys Run, crossing the stream many times in the descent, eventually emerging from the park in 5.4 miles and soon after connecting with VA611. Toward the end, Jeremys Run Trail connects with the Neighbor Mountain Trail to the east to form a 13.9-mile loop hike with the AT. Just after, Jeremys Run Trail also connects with the Knob Mountain Trail to form an 11.4-mile loop to the west.

Turn right on the Knob Mountain Cutoff Trail. The trail swings right and drops to a ford of Jeremys Run. You'll then begin a steep ascent of Knob Mountain with switchbacks. Near the top, you'll pass through a gap in a long rock fence that once enclosed a field or marked a boundary. You'll then curve to the right to a junction at 1.3 miles at the crest of the ridge where the Knob Mountain Trail follows an old roadway. To the left in 2.2 miles stands one of the summits of the mountain. Turn right toward the Mathews Arm Campground.

The old roadway ascends as it winds its way up the ridge, eventually curving right to swing around the taller summit of Knob Mountain. At 2.8 miles, you'll emerge on a road that leads down from the Mathews Arm Campground to a water treatment plant to the left. Turn right up the road. Soon after, the Heiskell Hollow Trail joins the road on the left. Stay on the road.

At 3.2 miles, you'll connect with a turnaround and parking area for access from the campground to the Knob Mountain Trail. Walk up the road into the campground to turn right on the entrance road past the registration building. Then watch for the Elkwallow Trail to turn off the road on the right at 3.4 miles.

The trail first follows an old roadway up from the paved road, but in a few paces turns off the roadway on a path to the right. The trail winds down to skirt the small stream that runs out of the campground and then follows the stream down in a steep descent to a boardwalk crossing of the upper reaches of Jeremys Run at 3.7 miles. Up from the creek crossing, the trail merges with an old roadway and parallels Skyline Drive, which is out of sight, to a junction with the AT at 4.7 miles.

At this junction, the AT to the left crosses Skyline Drive to head north. Straight ahead, you can reach the Elkwallow Wayside in another 0.1 mile. To complete this loop hike, turn right on the AT. The trail descends and then climbs to intersect with the Jeremys Run Trail and close the loop at 5.2 miles. Turn left to get back to parking at the Elkwallow Picnic Area.

Skyline Drive: At Mile 24.2, you'll pass the one-way road emerging from the Elkwallow Picnic Area.

⑲ Thornton River Trail

4.9 miles one-way
(Thornton River 1.5 miles one-way)
Moderate
Elevation loss: 1200 ft.
Cautions: Stream fords
Connections: Appalachian Trail, Hull School Trail

Attractions: The trail descends along the North Fork of the Thornton River, offering a pleasant stroll through an area once populated by mountaineers.

Trailhead: Turn in the trailhead parking on the east side of Skyline Drive at 25.4 miles. Just to the south of this parking area, the Thornton River Trail heads west up the slope to connect with the AT in 0.3 mile. For this hike, you'll take the Thornton River Trail east down the ridge following an old road that begins at the left side of the parking area.

Description: Descend along the old dirt road, which curves left below the parking area and then continues to descend into Thornton Hollow. At 0.1 mile you'll rockhop a small stream.

At 0.5 mile the road curves left and passes a spring on the left at 0.6 mile. Watch for a pile of rocks to the left at 0.8 mile that's the first sign of former human habitation in the hollow. The numerous rock piles you'll see in the woods remain from the clearing of fields for growing crops.

You'll cross a small stream from a spring at 1.0 mile, and then at 1.1 miles the trail passes an old rusted car abandoned on the left. Soon after, watch for the trail to turn left.

The hollow is wide and covered with thick grass dotted with pink, white, and yellow flowers along a small stream that is a tributary of the Thornton River. The trail could become over-grown in late summer. At 1.3 miles you'll cross another small stream from a spring to the left.

To the right at 1.4 miles, notice the small tributary you have been following joins the North Fork of the Thornton River. At

1.5 miles, you'll pass through rock walls and turn down right to ford the Thornton River.

The trail continues to follow the Thornton River, fording the stream three times before reaching a junction with the Hull School Trail at 3.1 miles; Hull School once stood near this intersection. To the left, the Hull School Trail ascends to a junction with the Fork Mountain Trail in 0.7 mile. To the right, the Hull School Trail ascends 2.2 miles to Skyline Drive at Mile 28.2.

The Thornton River Trail continues straight from the junction with the Hull School Trail to emerge from the park at 4.9 miles along an old road that becomes VA612; parking is very limited there.

Skyline Drive: From Jeremys Run Overlook at Mile 26.4, you'll have a view of the valley of Jeremys Run bordered by Neighbor Mountain on the left and Knob Mountain on the right. At Mile 26.8, paved parking on the west provides access to connecting trails to the Neighbor Mountain Trail and the Appalachian Trail.

From the Thornton Hollow Overlook at Mile 27.6 you'll have a view to the east; on the far left you'll see Piney Ridge running down into Thornton Hollow below; Pignut Mountain stands behind the ridge. The mountain in mid-view is Fork Mountain; to the right but more distant is Oventop; and farther to the right stands Pass Mountain.

At Mile 28.2, you'll find paved parking on the east for the Hull School Trail, which descends northeast, connecting with the Thornton River, Fork Mountain, and Piney Branch Trails, and beyond, connects with the Keyser Run Fire Road. Across the Drive from the Hull School Trail, a service road heads up the mountain to the Byrds Nest #4 day-use shelter.

②⓪ Byrds Nest #4 Loop

2.5 miles
Moderate
Elevation change: 300 ft.
Cautions: Steep ascent
Connections: Neighbor Mountain Trail,
Hull School Trail, Appalachian Trail

Attractions: This short loop takes you by Byrds Nest #4 day-use shelter.

Trailhead: Start at Beahms Gap at Mile 28.5 where you'll find parking on the west side of Skyline Drive.

Description: On the north end of the parking area at Beahms Gap, named for a family that entered the region around 1750, take the trail leading into the woods, which descends to the Appalachian Trail at 0.1 mile. Turn right on the AT.

At 0.2 mile, the trail crosses an old roadway marked by rows of rocks on your left. Just beyond, there's a spring off to your left. Just beyond that, you'll reach a junction with the AT left, and a connector trail straight. For this loop hike, you'll return on the AT from the left. For now, stay straight on the connector trail.

You'll ascend to connect with the service road up to Byrds Nest #4 at 0.4 mile. To the right on the service road, you can descend 0.1 mile to emerge on Skyline Drive across from the access to the Hull School Trail. Turn left on the service road, which is also the Neighbor Mountain Trail. You'll make a steep ascent to enter a clearing at 0.8 mile where you'll find Byrds Nest #4 day-use shelter. There are four such shelters in the park; the money for their construction was donated by Harry F. Byrd, Sr., who was Virginia's governor during the formation of the park and led the effort to raise funds for the purchase of the land; he was later U.S. Senator from Virginia. Byrds Nest #4 was built in 1965.

The Neighbor Mountain Trail passes beside the shelter on the right to ascend over the ridge and begin a descent of the moun-

Byrds Nest #4

tain on the other side. At 1.3 miles you'll descend to a junction where a side trail leads to the right 0.3 mile to reach Skyline Drive and trail access parking at Mile 26.8. Stay straight on the Neighbor Mountain Trail.

At 1.4 miles, you'll reach an intersection with the AT. To the right, you can descend steeply to reach the trail access parking on Skyline at Mile 26.8; a short trail connects the AT with the parking area at the same point at which the Neighbor Mountain Trail connector reaches the parking area. The Neighbor Mountain Trail continues straight from the junction with the AT to run out along the ridge of Neighbor Mountain, topping the summit, and then bearing north to descend off the mountain to a junction with the Jeremys Run Trail in 4.6 miles. The Neighbor Mountain and Jeremys Run Trails and the AT can be combined for a 13.9-mile loop hike.

At the intersection of the Neighbor Mountain Trail and the Appalachian Trail, turn left to follow the AT to the southeast to complete this short loop hike.

The AT passes over a knoll and begins a descent off the ridge of Neighbor Mountain. You'll descend into a saddle between Neighbor Mountain and Byrds Nest Summit and then bear to the right around the summit while descending through numerous large rock outcrops. At 2.3 miles, you'll close the loop at the junction with the connector trail left that leads to the Neighbor Mountain Trail where it coincides with the Byrds Nest #4 service road. Turn right on the AT back to Beahms Gap at 2.5 miles. You can also continue on the AT around the parking area at Beahms Gap to emerge on Skyline Drive just to the south of the parking area, which will add another 0.1 mile to your walk.

21 Pass Mountain

1.0 mile one-way
Moderate
Elevation gain: 550 ft.
Cautions: Steady ascent
Connections: Rocky Branch Trail, Appalachian Trail

Attractions: You'll reach the summit of Pass Mountain with views to the west.

Trailhead: Begin at Beahms Gap parking at Mile 28.5.

Description: Just to the south of the gap parking, pick up the Appalachian Trail where it crosses Skyline Drive. On the east side of the Drive follow the AT as it continues south.

At 0.1 mile, the AT crosses the Rocky Branch Trail. To the left, this trail travels 0.4 mile to emerge at the parking for the Hull School Trail on Skyline Drive at Mile 28.2. To the right, the Rocky Branch Trail continues south to cross Skyline Drive and reach the park boundary in 2.8 miles on VA666.

Continue straight on the AT through the intersection with the Rocky Branch Trail. Soon the trail curves right and begins an ascent of Pass Mountain. As the trail winds its way up the mountain, it doglegs to the right at 0.6 mile and then again at 0.7 mile. The trail is then somewhat level. As you begin ascending again, the AT makes another dogleg to the right, closer to the edge of the mountain.

Just as you top a shoulder of the mountain, the trail passes through rocks at 0.9 mile. There's some view through the trees, but stay on the trail to the far end of the outcrop to where a path leads right to a view to the west of Kemp Hollow with Neighbor Mountain to the right and Knob Mountain beyond.

Across this second shoulder, the AT then switchbacks up through rocks to the summit of Pass Mountain at 1.0 mile. The AT swings left across the summit, and then begins a descent of the other side of Pass Mountain. At 1.8 miles, you would reach the Pass Mountain Trail that descends east past the Pass Mountain

Hut and emerges in 3 miles on US211 east of Thornton Gap; there is some parking across the highway.

The AT continues past the Pass Mountain Trail to descend into Thornton Gap at 3.1 miles.

Skyline Drive: At Mile 30.1 on Skyline Drive, you'll reach the Pass Mountain Overlook that offers a view down Kemp Hollow with Neighbor Mountain to the right. You'll see Massanutten in the distance marked with the notch of New Market Gap. US211 runs from the gap across the valley to Luray below. From the overlook, a 0.2-mile loop trail begins straight out and circles left to return through a gap in the fence to the left.

Continuing on Skyline Drive, you'll pass the service road for the Pass Mountain Hut on the left at Mile 31.4, just as you enter Thornton Gap; the AT follows this service road down into Thornton Gap to cross the Drive here and descend to cross US211 and pass below the Panorama complex. As you drive into the gap, notice Mary's Rock at the peak of the mountain on the other side.

US211 divides the North District of the park from the Central District. To your left as you enter the gap from the north stands the Thornton Gap entrance station. The gap bears the name of Francis Thornton who owned much land and a mansion and mill to the east in the early 1700s. The road through Thornton Gap was built in 1746, one of the first roads to cross the Blue Ridge. Andrew Russell Barbee later operated it as a toll road and took in lodgers at his home, Hawsburg, located in the gap. At the time the park was established, there was a Panorama Hotel and Restaurant in the gap. The name "Panorama" apparently dates from another of the Barbee houses. Now there's the Panorama Restaurant and Giftshop built in the 1960s and operated by the concessionaire. At times, park information and backcountry camping permits are available at the small building to the front, which is only intermittently staffed.

To the west on US211, you'll find a number of bed & breakfasts, such as Jordon Hollow Farm in Stanley and The Mayne View in Luray. Also in Luray, stands The Mimslyn, the grand old inn of Virginia. On the east side of the park, you'll find additional services in Sperryville.

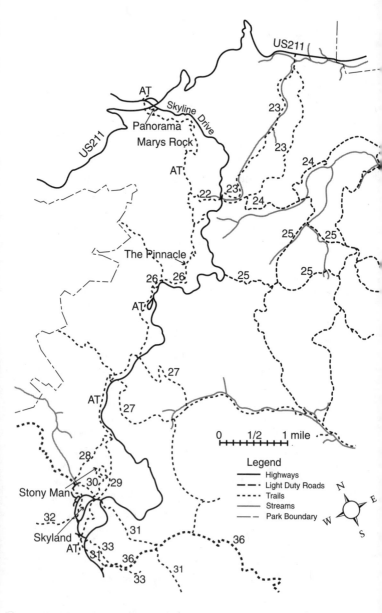

Map 5. Marys Rock to Skyland

22 Meadow Spring Trail

0.7 mile one-way
(Marys Rock 1.4 miles one-way)
Moderate
Elevation gain: 600 ft.
Cautions: Steep ascent, drop-offs
Connections: Buck Hollow Trail,
Hazel Mountain Trail, Appalachian Trail

Attractions: Marys Rock on the AT, just north of the Meadow Spring Trail, provides a panoramic view of Thornton Gap.

Trailhead: You can reach Marys Rock along the AT from the Panorama complex in Thornton Gap; at the end of the upper parking lot, you'll find a short connector trail to the AT, which you can then take north for a steep ascent of the mountain, reaching Marys Rock in 1.7 miles.

For access to a shorter hike, continue up Skyline Drive. At Mile 32.2, you'll pass through 600-foot Marys Rock Tunnel. From the Tunnel Parking Overlook at Mile 32.4 on the east, you'll see Thornton River Hollow below with Oventop Mountain to the left and Skinner Ridge to the right. Out through the hollow lies Sperryville, near where the Thornton Mill once stood.

At the Buck Hollow Overlook on the east at Mile 32.9, Skinner Ridge lies below with Buck Hollow to the right and Buck Ridge farther to the right; you can just see Hazel Mountain over Buck Ridge. At the Hazel Mountain Overlook at Mile 33.0, you can climb up granodiorite boulders for a view across Buck Hollow to Buck Ridge with Hazel Mountain on the other side.

Turn in the Meadow Spring Parking Area at Mile 33.5, which also gives access to the Buck Hollow and Hazel Mountain Trails.

Description: From the parking area on the east side of the road, walk north up Skyline Drive 100 yards and cross to the beginning of the Meadow Spring Trail, marked by a post on the west side of the road. You'll pass a stream on the right descending from Meadow Spring.

The trail leads into the woods in a steep ascent. Watch for blooming laurel and azalea in spring and stands of cinnamon fern. At 0.4 mile, you'll pass the foundation and chimney for a backcountry cabin that burned in the 1940s. At 0.7 mile, you'll ascend to a junction with the Appalachian Trail. To the left, you would pass Byrds Nest #3 Shelter in 0.6 mile and reach Skyland in 7.1 miles. Byrds Nest #3 was built in 1963 with funds provided by Senator Harry F. Byrd, Sr. Turn right to get to Marys Rock.

You'll have a view from rocks to the left at 1.1 miles. Continuing north, the AT curves around a rock monolith at 1.3 miles and reaches a junction soon after with the AT turning right and a left side path leading to Marys Rock. Turn left here and ascend to Marys Rock at 1.4 miles. Standing on the bare rock of the summit, old rock of Pedlar granodiorite, you'll have a view of Thornton Gap 1200 feet below. Marys Rock was named for either the daughter of Frances Thornton or the wife of William Randolph Barbee, son of Andrew Barbee, who took over the toll road from his father and was later a famous sculptor, as was his son, Herbert.

From Marys Rock you can either return the way you came to the Meadow Spring Parking Area, or if you have a vehicle to pick you up at Thornton Gap, you can descend on the AT. In making the descent, you'll drop below rock monoliths at 2.1 miles, walk some sections of trail shored up with stone, and make several switchbacks to reach a junction at 3.1 miles. The AT heads straight through Thornton Gap to continue north. The trail to the right leads 30 yards out to the upper parking lot at the Panorama Restaurant.

Marys Rock

23 Buck Hollow/ Buck Ridge Loop

5.6 miles
Moderate, difficult ascent
Elevation change: 1750 ft.
Cautions: Steep descent and ascent, stream fords
Connections: Meadow Spring Trail,
Hazel Mountain Trail

Attractions: This loop hike descends along a pretty stream with boulders and cascades and then ascends along a ridge with views of Thornton Gap.

Trailhead: Begin at the Meadow Spring Parking Area at Mile 33.5 on Skyline Drive.

Description: At the right end of the parking area, where the Hazel Mountain Trail heads straight down an old road, the Buck Hollow Trail turns off left to pass behind the parking area. The trail soon swings right and heads straight out, descending gently. At 0.1 mile the trail skirts on the right the stream that flows down from Meadow Spring.

You'll descend more steeply at 0.3 mile as the stream drops more rapidly down Buck Hollow. At 0.7 mile the trail turns right, and you'll rockhop the now tumbling stream. As the trail continues downstream, you'll pass several cascades; watch for a multi-step drop in the streambed at 1.0 mile.

The trail stays up for a time and then at 1.1 miles curves right to begin the descent again. The trail becomes steep and rocky as it winds down into the hollow.

Back along the creek, watch for a natural water slide in the streambed at 1.7 miles. At 1.8 miles, the trail swings right to cross a side stream and immediately turns left to ford the main stream; do not go straight on an old roadbed.

As you continue to descend along the stream, now on the left side, you'll cross wet-weather streams and springs. Watch for early spring wildflowers, sprinklings of blue hepatica. At 2.5 miles, bear left across a shallow side stream, which may be dry in summer, to continue down a rocky section of trail. Swing right and ford the main creek, which has grown larger, at 2.7 miles.

At 2.8 miles you'll reach a junction with the Buck Ridge Trail to the right. The Buck Hollow Trail continues along the creek to ford it again and then ford the Thornton River and emerge on US211; there's a pulloff and room to park a few cars on this east side of the Blue Ridge down from Thornton Gap

To complete the loop hike, take the sharp right onto the Buck Ridge Trail. You'll cross a side stream and walk up a rocky and usually dry streambed and then bear left out of the streambed to begin a steep ascent of Buck Ridge at 2.9 miles. You'll soon bear right and keep climbing in a long, tough ascent that's about as steep as it gets without having to use your hands to pull yourself up.

At 3.0 miles, you'll reach the ridgeline and continue in a more gentle ascent, with some steep sections. The dry ridgeline has a pine, laurel, and oak forest.

At 3.9 miles, the trail swings to the north side of the ridge where you'll step down a rock outcrop that's a perfect resting place offering a view through the trees of Thornton Gap; Skinner Ridge lies to the left and Pass Mountain stands across the gap with Oventop Mountain to the right. As you continue around the bluff, you'll be looking at Marys Rock over Skinner Ridge. You'll soon swing left back to the ridgeline and continue the ascent.

You'll top a shoulder of the ridge at 4.1 miles and continue along the ridgeline with Skinner Ridge to the right and Hazel Mountain to the left. At 4.5 miles, the trail makes a winding ascent of a rocky slope. Soon, a side path leads to a limited view east. At 4.6 miles, the trail curves across bare rock through an open area that offers winter views through leafless trees.

Later, skirting to the left of the ridgeline, you'll reach a junction at 5.1 miles with an old road that's the Hazel Mountain Trail. Turn right. You'll return to the Meadow Spring Parking area to close the loop at 5.6 miles.

24 Hazel Mountain/ White Rocks Loop

8.4 miles
(waterfall 2.5 miles one-way)
(White Rocks 3.0 miles one-way)
Moderate
Elevation change: 1400 ft.
Cautions: Steep descent to waterfall, stream crossings
Connections: Meadow Spring Trail, Buck Hollow and Buck
Ridge Trails, Hazel River Trail

Attractions: Once on the White Rocks Trail, you'll have access to a waterfall and the White Rocks.

Trailhead: The Hazel Mountain Trail begins at the Meadow Spring Parking Area at Mile 33.5 on Skyline Drive.

Description: The Hazel Mountain Trail follows an old road just to the right of the parking area on the east side of the Drive. Immediately, the Buck Hollow Trail turns off to the left to pass below the parking area and head north. Stay straight on the old road past a chain gate. The water from Meadow Spring runs under the trail in a culvert.

Descending along the road, you'll reach a junction with the Buck Ridge Trail to the left at 0.5 mile. The Hazel Mountain Trail bears to the right.

As you continue to descend, the footing becomes rocky on the old roadway. At 0.7 mile the road curves left, and at 1.1 miles, curves back right. At 1.4 miles, you'll see a stream off to the right, a tributary of the Hazel River. At 1.5 miles, you'll rock-hop a side stream of this tributary and pass a hemlock woods along the creek. You'll reach a junction at 1.6 miles with the White Rocks Trail to the left. The Hazel Mountain Trail continues straight, giving access to several backcountry trails and ending at a junction with the Pine Hill Gap Trail in another 2.9 miles. Turn left onto the White Rocks Trail.

You'll ascend up another old roadway that is the Old Hazel Road, crossing a small stream and reaching a dry ridge of oak and laurel. The trail gradually bears right and begins a descent along the ridgeline. Across the valley of the Hazel River, you'll see Hazel Mountain off to the right. At 2.4 miles, you'll see a path to the right that hikers have made looking for the waterfall; but this is not the trail to the falls. Continue descending on the old roadway. At 2.5 miles you'll reach a more worn path to the right that gives access to the waterfall; when we were last there, a tree snag with a trail blaze stood at the junction.

Although the walk to this junction has been easy, the path down to the waterfall is difficult. You'll need to be agile to make the steep descent to the Hazel River and then to make your way upstream to the falls, a picturesque eight-foot falls that's worth the 0.2-mile scramble. At the falls, you'll see an overhang to the right with a crevice going a few feet into the rock.

Back on the main trail, continue down the old road. You'll pass exposed boulders and dip through a saddle to then make an ascent of the first of three knolls along the ridge. At 2.8 miles, you'll reach the top of the first knoll and then descend the other side. Hazel Mountain stands mightily to the right, and you'll hear the Hazel River below. Through another saddle and up the second knoll, watch for large patches of trailing arbutus. You'll have nice views left across the valley to Buck Ridge.

The trail skirts to the left of the peak of the second knoll, which is topped by the White Rocks, exposed Old Rag Granite. You'll only catch a glimpse of the rocks from the trail. But keep going, and on the other side of the knoll, just before the trail begins the descent into the next saddle, a path to the right at 3.0 miles takes you up into the giant exposed boulders.

The White Rocks Trail continues down and then over a third knoll before turning right to descend off the ridge. The trail then crosses the Hazel River and a tributary to connect with the Hazel River Trail at 3.9 miles. Turn right up the Hazel River Trail to reconnect with the Hazel Mountain Trail at 5.5 miles. Turning right, you'll close the loop at the beginning of the White Rocks Trail at 6.8 miles, along the way fording Runyon Run, passing the Catlett Spur Trail to the left, and crossing the Hazel River on a bridge. It's then 1.6 miles back to Meadow Spring Parking.

25 Hannah Run/Catlett Mountain Loop

6.4 miles
Moderate
Elevation change: 1100 ft.
Cautions: Stream crossings
Connections: Hazel Mountain Trail, Hazel River Trail,
Sams Ridge/Broad Hollow Trails

Attractions: This fine loop hike introduces you to a section of the Shenandoah wilderness.

Trailhead: Along Skyline Drive, you'll pass the service road for Byrds Nest Shelter #3 on the west at Mile 33.9. Turn in the Pinnacles Overlook on the east at Mile 35.1, which offers a view of Hannah Run Valley below, framed by Catlett Mountain to the left and Pinnacle Ridge to the right with Old Rag Mountain in the background. Look to the far left of the parking area for a trailhead post and a break in the rock wall. You'll descend stone steps there and bear left to begin the Hannah Run Trail.

Description: Descending a few yards, the trail switchbacks right through some rocks, but soon turns left. Hiking the trail in the fall, you'll find bright leaves littering the ground like the remains of a parade that has passed through.

The trail winds down the ridge, dips through a couple of coves, and then heads out onto a ridge. You'll descend from the ridge and switchback left to a junction at 1.2 miles. Here the Hannah Run Trail continues to the right to connect with the Nicholson Hollow Trail in another 2.5 miles. For this loop hike, turn left onto the Catlett Mountain Trail.

At 1.3 miles, you'll reach a second junction where the Catlett Mountain Trail continues straight. To walk this loop clockwise, turn left here on the Catlett Spur Trail. This trail follows an old roadway, on and off. At 1.9 miles, you'll pass a hemlock grove on the left.

At 2.0 miles at Runyon Run, a tributary of the Hazel River, turn right downstream. The trail crosses a small tributary where it joins the creek. You'll then rockhop the main stream at 2.1 miles and turn downstream. The trail crosses a small tributary and passes through a wet area where a spring emerges on the left. Watch for rows and piles of rocks along a section of old roadway, evidence of past settlement. You'll descend to a junction beside Runyon Run at 2.4 miles with the Hazel Mountain Trail. Straight, the Hazel Mountain Trail ascends back to Skyline Drive, passing the White Rocks Trail.

Turn right on the Hazel Mountain Trail to ford Runyon Run and head up an old road along a tributary. You'll ascend steeply to reach a junction at 3.4 miles with the Hazel River Trail to the left; that trail descends along the Hazel River, passing the other end of the White Rocks Trail, to emerge from the park and connect with VA600 in 2.8 miles. Stay straight on the Hazel Mountain Trail to a junction with the Sams Ridge/Broad Hollow Trail at 3.5 miles. To the left these two trails separate in 0.2 mile, and each descends the ridge. Continue up the old roadway.

You'll descend to a junction with the Catlett Mountain Trail at 4.0 miles. The Hazel Mountain Trail continues straight to end at junctions with the Hot Mtn.-Short Mtn. and the Pine Hill Gap Trails. Turn right on the Catlett Mountain Trail.

The trail descends through pine and hemlock. At 4.1 miles, a wagon wheel rim lay on the ground between two stream crossings when we last hiked through here. The trail ascends from these streams. At 4.2 miles, notice rock piles to the left that mark the site of a house or field. The trail then bears right to wind uphill.

After crossing this spur ridge of Catlett Mountain, the trail descends, skirts left around a sinkhole, and closes the loop at the junction with the Catlett Spur Trail at 5.1 miles. Stay straight to reach the Hannah Run Trail at 5.2 miles. Turn right to return to Skyline Drive at the Pinnacles Overlook at 6.4 miles.

Skyline Drive: From the Pinnacle Overlook south on the Skyline Drive, the pinxter-flower is especially plentiful and the pink blossoms beautiful in late May.

26 The Pinnacle

1.2 miles one-way
Moderate
Elevation gain: 350 ft.
Cautions: Rocky in places
Connections: Appalachian Trail, Leading Ridge Trail

Attractions: A short hike on the Appalachian Trail takes you to the top of The Pinnacle.

Trailhead: Pull in the Jewell Hollow Overlook at Mile 36.4 and park at the back of the second parking area. The view is of Tutweiler Hollow straight out from the overlook, bounded by Leading Ridge on the right. The valley beyond Leading Ridge is Jewell Hollow.

Description: At the back of the parking area, you'll find a 50-foot path that connects with the Appalachian Trail. The Pinnacles Picnic Area is 0.3 mile to the left along the AT. Turn right to hike to The Pinnacle.

The AT descends right and left down to a broad shelf that it traverses below the overlook parking area. At 0.2 mile you'll pass a side path to the right that offers a second way for you to access the AT from the overlook, this one from the first parking area.

The trail then passes through an open area with a view down Tutweiler Hollow. Back into the woods, you'll begin an ascent of Leading Ridge. At 0.3 mile, you'll reach an intersection with the Leading Ridge Trail. To the right, the trail emerges on Skyline Drive in 0.1 mile at Mile 36.2; to the left, the trail leads out Leading Ridge to dead-end at the park boundary in 1.2 miles.

From Leading Ridge continue ascending along the AT, passing through a laurel thicket. At 0.7 mile, you'll ascend among huge granodiorite boulders of the Pedlar formation. A pile of boulders on the left at 0.8 mile has one about 15 feet high standing on end. You'll soon pass over a shoulder of the ridge and continue along the ridgeline. At 1.0 mile the trail passes over the first summit of The Pinnacle. The trail descends a little, where you'll pass more boulders standing on end. You'll then ascend over the northern summit of The Pinnacle, the fifth highest peak in the park at 3730 feet.

The AT begins a descent from The Pinnacle with switchbacks right and left. At 1.2 miles, after the AT turns right again, watch for a path on the left that leads out to a point surrounded in trees. You can climb up on rocks for a view north to Marys Rock and to the northwest down Jewell Hollow with Neighbor Mountain in the distance. From here, the AT continues to descend, passing Byrds Nest Shelter #3 in another 0.8 mile and a junction with the Meadow Spring Trail in 0.6 mile beyond the shelter.

Skyline Drive: At Mile 36.7 lies the Pinnacles Picnic Area on the west. The AT skirts the back end of the picnic area; a hundred yards south on the AT you'll reach a viewpoint that has become overgrown, at least, when we were last there.

27 Corbin Cabin/ Nicholson Hollow Loop

4.2 miles
Moderate
Elevation change: 1050 ft.
Cautions: Steep descent and ascent, rocky
Connections: Appalachian Trail, Indian Run Trail,
Crusher Ridge Trail

Attractions: This short loop takes you by the historic Corbin Cabin and provides access to the backcountry.

Trailhead: Pull in the parking area on the west side of Skyland Drive at Mile 37.9.

Description: At the south end of the parking area, a path leads a short distance to the AT; this will be your return route. To start the hike, walk across Skyline Drive and pick up the Corbin Cabin Cutoff Trail.

The trail descends through the woods with mountain laurel, pinxter-flower, and patches of pink lady's slipper; we nicknamed this first part of the path the "Pink Trail." You'll make a steep descent, curving left at 0.6 mile and turning down right along a small stream at 0.7 mile. Watch for a large oak tree on the left at 0.8 mile.

At 1.0 mile, you'll see evidence of former human habitation, a rock pile from a cleared field on the right. At 1.1 miles, a collapsed chimney on the left marks a former housesite. Soon after on the right, you'll see a rock wall and beyond a collapsed log cabin. The trail passes more rock piles and rock walls. At 1.2 miles, you'll pass the end of a rock wall and soon rockhop a small creek and curve up right to pass more rock walls.

You'll see a ruined cabin off to the right and then drop to ford the Hughes River and walk up to a junction with the Nicholson Hollow Trail in front of Corbin Cabin at 1.4 miles. The cabin, built by George Corbin in 1909, is one of the last remaining examples of the mountaineer cabins. After the park was established, the cabin stood empty until the Potomac Appalachian Trail Club restored the structure in the 1950s. The PATC maintains the cabin; it may be rented for overnight stays.

To the left, the Nicholson Hollow Trail descends along the Hughes River into Nicholson Hollow. Several families here once formed "Free State Hollow," where they were free to govern their own lives since the law feared to enter. Aaron Nicholson, the patriarch of the community, was by most accounts a formidable person with his white beard and piercing blue eyes. The Nicholson Hollow Trail passes junctions with the Hannah Run and Hot Mountain-Short Mountain Trails to emerge from the park and join the Weakley Hollow Fire Road in 4.0 miles from Corbin Cabin.

To complete this loop back to Skyline Drive, turn right on the Nicholson Hollow Trail at Corbin Cabin. Heading upstream along the Hughes River, you'll walk up to a junction with the Indian Run Trail at 1.6 miles. To the left, the Indian Run Trail connects this upper end of the Nicholson Hollow Trail with the Corbin Mountain Trail in 1.7 miles, with access then to Old Rag Fire Road to the west. The Corbin Mountain Trail circles east to connect with the lower part of the Nicholson Hollow Trail. These trails offer opportunities for several longer backcountry hikes.

For this hike, continue straight up the Nicholson Hollow Trail from this junction with the Indian Run Trail. The trail follows an old road through here. You'll ford Indian Run, a tributary of the Hughes River, at 1.7 miles. Watch for a large oak on the right at 2.0 miles. The trail then follows a creek on the left to begin a steep rocky climb back up the ridge. You'll pass a spring at 2.8 miles. After more steep uphill hiking, you'll emerge on Skyline Drive at 3.2 miles. Turn left to walk along the Drive for 100 yards to pick up an old roadway on the west side of the Drive. Walking into the woods, you'll reach a junction with the Crusher Ridge Trail to the right at 3.3 miles. Bear left to reach the AT at 3.4 miles. Now turn right to head back to the beginning of the loop.

The AT leads uphill to curve right over a ridge and reach an intersection with the Crusher Ridge Trail at 3.6 miles. To the right, that trail descends to the previous junction. To the left, the

Crusher Ridge Trail heads out along Crusher Ridge, eventually to descend to the park boundary where it dead-ends in 1.7 miles. Continue straight on the AT. The trail switchbacks downhill, rises, and then drops again to reach the side trail at 4.2 miles that leads right to the parking area where you began the hike.

Skyline Drive: At Mile 38.4, the Nicholson Hollow Trail emerges on Skyline Drive from the east and then just beyond reenters the woods on the west side.

You'll then reach the Stony Man Mountain Overlook at Mile 38.6. Looking south you'll see the profile of Stony Man; the rock bluff on the mountain forms his brow; an outcrop serves as his nose; the trees down the slope form his flowing beard. When you hike to the summit of Stony Man Mountain, you'll be standing on a rock ledge at the top of his forehead. Straight out from this overlook, you'll see the town of Luray and, beyond, New Market Gap in Massanutten Mountain. North from the overlook, you'll see The Pinnacle. A short trail at the southern end of the parking area leads past restrooms to connect with the AT.

28 Passamaquoddy Trail

1.8 miles one-way
(Lower Little Stony Man 0.5 mile one-way)
Moderate
Elevation gain: 500 ft.
Cautions: Rocky
Connections: Appalachian Trail, Skyland Road,
Bushytop Trail

Attractions: This route gives quick access to the lower ledge of Little Stony Man and forms a good loop hike with the AT.

Trailhead: At Mile 39.1, pull in the parking area on the west, which gives access to the Appalachian Trail.

Description: From the parking area, head up the rocky trail into the woods to a junction with the Appalachian Trail in 50 yards. Turn left to head south on the AT. The trail curves left and passes above Skyline Drive. At 0.3 mile, you'll switchback right and ascend to a junction at 0.4 mile with the Passamaquoddy Trail. To the left, the AT ascends to Little Stony Man Cliffs in another 0.2 mile. Stay straight on the Passamaquoddy, an Indian word meaning "abounding in pollock"; the trail was built by George Freeman Pollock and named to honor his parents.

At 0.5 mile you'll emerge on the lower ledge of the Little Stony Man Cliffs with good views of the valley. The trail passes below the upper cliff of Little Stony Man and then penetrates a hemlock wood to pass under a powerline at 1.3 miles and reach Furnace Spring on the left. A copper smelter was located here that handled the ore once mined on Stony Man Mountain. Now the spring supplies water for Skyland. You'll see water emerging below the trail.

Just beyond the spring, you'll reach a junction with the Skyland Road at 1.4 miles that gave access to the Skyland Resort before the park was established. To the right, the road descends the mountain and emerges from the park as VA672. Turn left up the road to another junction. To the left, you can pick up a horse trail that leads to the Stony Man Nature Trail parking area and can be used for a loop hike with the AT, returning to the parking area on Skyline Drive where you started (see Trail #29).

To complete the Passamaquoddy Trail stay straight up the road. You'll pass a steep service road on the left that dead-ends up the slope. Stay straight on the Skyland Road. At 1.5 miles, the Passamaquoddy Trail turns left off the road on a footpath. The road continues on up into the Skyland cabin area. Turning left up the trail, you'll pass behind the Skyland amphitheater and emerge on a paved road at 1.6 miles that leads left up toward the north entrance of Skyland; the cabin area is to the right. The trail crosses the road and continues up through the woods to a junction at 1.7 miles with a paved path that leads down from the dining room to the cabin area. Turn left up the paved path.

As the path swings right, a side path leads to an employees area. Just below the dining room at 1.8 miles, the trail turns off the paved path to follow a graveled path that passes below the lodge office, eventually connecting with the paved road on the other side of the complex at 2.0 miles. Across the road, you can pick up the Bushytop Trail to Millers Head.

Skyline Drive: From the Hemlock Springs Overlook at Mile 39.7, you'll have a view north into Nicholson Hollow with The Pinnacle to the left and Hazel and Catlett Mountains to the right. Hemlock Springs lies below the overlook, out of sight.

The view from the Thorofare Mountain Overlook at Mile 40.5 is probably the most photographed. A tall dead tree out from the overlook frames Old Rag Mountain in the distance, the exposed granite at the peak making it look ragged. Thorofare Mountain lies straight out from the overlook.

Thorofare Mountain Overlook

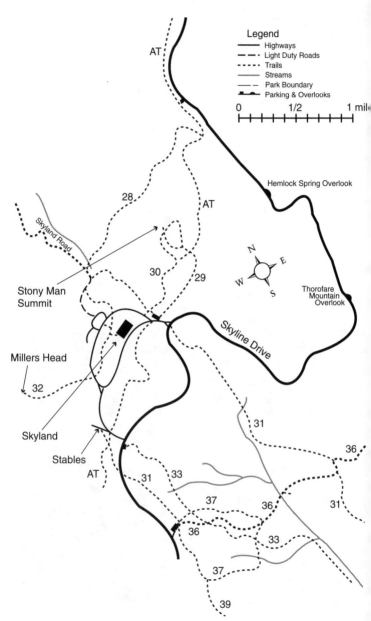

Map 6. Skyland Area

90

29 Stony Man Nature Trail

0.7 mile one-way
(Little Stony Man Cliffs 1.0 mile one-way)
Moderate
Elevation change: 400 ft.
Cautions: Steep ascent, rocky
Connections: Appalachian Trail, Stony Man Horse Trail

Attractions: The nature trail takes you to the summit of Stony Man Mountain, and a side trip on the AT takes you to the cliffs of Little Stony Man.

Trailhead: At Mile 41.7, turn in the north entrance to Skyland and immediately turn right into trailhead parking for the nature trail. From the south, the Appalachian Trail crosses the island between the south and north entrances to Skyland and enters the Stony Man parking area to pick up the nature trail.

Description: Head up the paved path at the right corner of the parking area and then bear right on the graveled path. The nature trail has numbered posts corresponding to a nature trail brochure available wherever books are sold in the park.

You'll begin an ascent through blooming pinxter-flower the end of May, first of June. At 0.2 mile, a bench sits on the right. Then at 0.4 mile you'll reach a junction. To the left lies a connector to the Stony Man Horse Trail. The Appalachian Trail, which has been following the nature trail, now turns off to the right, which will be the route to the cliffs of Little Stony Man; at this junction on Stony Man Mountain, the AT is at its highest point in the park. To reach the summit of Stony Man, continue straight up the mountain.

You'll reach a fork at 0.5 mile for a short loop over the summit. Stay right. You'll pass a view to the right of distant Nicholson Hollow on the east side of the ridge. The trail passes an old copper mine site on the left and reaches the summit at a four-way intersection at 0.7 mile. To the left is the return part of the summit loop; straight is the Stony Man Horse Trail. Turn right to get to the summit view in 70 yards, where you'll stand on bare rock to look westward to Shenandoah Valley. You are standing at the top of Stony Man's forehead, the profile visible from the Stony Man Overlook at Mile 38.6. The Stony Man Summit is the second highest peak in the park at 4011 feet.

Retracing your steps to the intersection, descend on the return portion of the summit loop to close the loop at the fork and descend to the junction with the AT to the left at a total of 1.0 mile. If you're just out for a walk to the summit, stay straight to return to the parking area at 1.4 miles. To get to Little Stony Man, turn left on the AT, headed north. The trail descends, emerging on the cliffs of Little Stony Man at 1.6 miles. If you look carefully below, you'll see the lower ledge of Little Stony Man Cliffs, traversed by the Passamaquoddy Trail.

You'll continue descending steeply with switchbacks to a junction at 1.8 miles with the Passamaquoddy Trail to the left. If you were to continue straight on the AT, you would reach in another 0.4 mile the Little Stony Man parking area on Skyline Drive at Mile 39.1.

You can walk a loop by turning left on the Passamaquoddy Trail to where it emerges on Skyland Road at a total of 2.8 miles (see Trail #28); then turn left up to a junction where you'll turn left on a side road that's open to horses. The side road becomes a trail, passing under a powerline and turning right steeply up the slope. At 3.6 miles, you'll reach the Stony Man Horse Trail. To the right the trail leads out to the paved road in 50 yards. Turn left to reach the nature trailhead parking on the right to complete the loop. The horse trail continues to the summit of Stony Man.

Skyline Drive: Skyland has grown from George Pollock's mountain retreat. Newer buildings house a restaurant/giftshop and registration. Visitor accommodations are in lodge buildings and small cabins on a lower shoulder of the mountain where Pollock's camp was located. Several of the old cabins still exist, including Massanutten Lodge, the 1911 home of Addie Nairn who later married Pollock. The only original cabin in which visitors can stay is Byrds Nest, the cabin of Governor/Senator Harry F. Byrd, Sr., a park supporter; the cabin had belonged to his father.

Stony Man

㉚ Stony Man Horse Trail

0.7 mile one-way
Moderate
Elevation gain: 400 ft.
Cautions: Steep ascent, rocky
Connections: Stony Man Nature Trail, Skyland Road,
Skyland-Big Meadows Horse Trail

Attractions: Horse riders have access on this trail to the summit of Stony Man Mountain.

Trailhead: At the far left end of the parking for the Stony Man Nature Trail at Mile 41.7, a path leads into the woods a few yards to give access to the Stony Man Horse Trail. The trail leads to the left 70 yards to emerge on the paved road. Just down this trail, you can reach the connector horse trail to the Skyland Road on the right (see Trail #29, end of description).

Description: Turn right on the Stony Man Horse Trail and begin a steep, rocky ascent of Stony Man Mountain. At 0.2 mile, the trail forks, with the right fork giving access to the nature trail in 100 yards, but only for hikers. Take the left fork to continue up toward the summit of Stony Man. You'll ascend to a bare rock overlook at 0.5 mile with Skyland laid out to the your left and a view to your right across the valley. Then at 0.6 mile, you'll reach a junction with the nature trail and the end of the horse trail. You can tie horses here to a hitching rail and walk 70 yards to the left to the summit and a repeat scene of the earlier view. There is no horse trail connection on the summit of Stony Man, so you must ride back down the mountain.

Past the parking area on the left and past the connector to the right that heads over to Skyland Road, you'd reach the paved road where you can turn left, riding along the road, to cross Skyline Drive and access the Skyland-Big Meadows Horse Trail. The Stony Man parking area is frequently used for loading and unloading horses because of this easy access to horse trails.

3̣1̣ Skyland-Big Meadows Horse Trail

11.3 miles one-way
Moderate
Elevation change: 1100 ft.
Cautions: Skyline Drive crossings, narrow and rocky in places
Connections: Stony Man Horse Trail, Old Rag Fire Road,
Limberlost Trail, Whiteoak Canyon Trail,
Whiteoak Fire Road, Cedar Run Trail, Rose River Loop,
Rose River Fire Road, Story-of-the-Forest Nature Trail,
Tanners Ridge Horse Trail

Attractions: This horse trail leaves Skyland for a long ride south to Big Meadows.

Trailhead: From the parking for Stony Man Horse Trail and Nature Trail, ride east along the side of the road 0.1 mile to Skyline Drive at the north entrance to Skyland at Mile 41.7. Cross the Drive and pick up the Skyland-Big Meadows Horse Trail on the east side. Concrete posts mark miles and half miles.

Description: The horse trail descends east from Skyline Drive to connect with the Old Rag Fire Road at 1.2 miles. Turn right on the road and then watch for the horse trail to turn off left back into the woods.

Alternative access to this horse trail leads from the stable area at the Skyland South Entrance to cross to the east side of Skyline Drive. After a little downhill, you'll pass through old apple and cherry orchards with deer browsing beneath the trees and grouse scurrying out of the way. At 0.4 mile, you'll cross the upper end of the Limberlost Trail and reach a junction with the Old Rag Fire Road. To the right is parking where you have access just off Skyline Drive for the Old Rag Fire Road and the Limberlost Trail. Turn east on Old Rag Road. You'll cross the Whiteoak Canyon Trail and continue down the road to enter "The Limberlost" hemlock forest. At 0.9 mile, you'll cross the lower section of the Limberlost Trail. The road soon descends to cross the upper stream of Whiteoak Run. At 1.5 miles, you'll reach a junction with the horse trail turning right off the road. The fire road continues east toward Old Rag Mountain, and just up the road is where the northern access for the Skyland-Big Meadows Horse Trail joins the road. The two access routes meet here where the horse trail turns south off Old Rag Road.

Now follow a graveled path through the woods. Watch for a large snag on the right and a huge oak and then large hemlocks at 2.0 miles. At 2.5 miles, you'll descend steeply to reach a junction with the Whiteoak Canyon Trail at 3.0 miles. Just to the right, you'll find hitching rails where you can leave your horse and walk down the hiking trail to the left for 0.1 mile to a high overlook of the upper falls of Whiteoak Run.

From the hitching rails, continue right to a ford of Whiteoak Run. This is the lowest point on the horse trail; from here you'll ascend toward Big Meadows. On the other side of Whiteoak Run, pick up the Whiteoak Fire Road.

At 4.7 miles, the horse trail turns off left. Skyline Drive at Mile 45.0 is just 0.1 mile up the road, but to continue toward Big Meadows, turn left on the trail, narrow and rocky. Watch for stinging nettle. At 5.2 miles, you'll reach a junction with the Cedar Run Trail. To the right, it's 50 yards up to Hawksbill Gap on the Drive at Mile 45.6. Stay straight on the horse trail.

At 6.6 miles, a side trail right leads out to the Upper Hawksbill Parking on the Drive at Mile 46.7. Bear left to continue south on the horse trail. You'll cross the headwaters of the Rose River. At 9.1 miles the Rose River Loop joins the horse trail from the left. The two coincide to the Rose River Fire Road at 9.6 miles. The road leads right to Skyline Drive at Fishers Gap at Mile 49.4. The horse trail crosses Rose River Fire Road to the left and then crosses Skyline Drive to the west side at 9.7 miles.

The trail parallels Skyline Drive on the west, eventually entering the Big Meadows area and crossing the Story-of-the-Forest Nature Trail at 11.0 miles. You'll then reach a junction at 11.2 miles. To the left lies a maintenance area that has a corral, but it's no longer open to the public. Turn right for 0.1 mile to reach a side trail left to parking for the Tanners Ridge Horse Trail; a frequently used area for loading and unloading horses.

32 Bushytop/Millers Head Trail

0.8 mile one-way
(Bushytop Overlook 0.2 mile one-way)
Moderate
Elevation loss: 300 ft.
Cautions: Rocky in places
Connections: Passamaquoddy Trail

Attractions: This short walk takes you past Bushytop Overlook and out to Millers Head for a panoramic view east; an essential hike for those staying at Skyland.

Trailhead: Turn in the south entrance to Skyland at Mile 42.5. You'll pass the stables on the left where you can take guided horse rides; the AT crosses the road near the stables. Continue straight where you would turn right to the restaurant/registration area. You'll soon descend into the lodging complex. The trail to Bushytop and Millers Head begins on the left, across from the Franklin and Winchester lodges; look for a trail post. If you are not staying at Skyland, you'll need to look for parking in this vicinity. Among the lodge buildings on the right, the Passamaquoddy Trail leads up to the Skyland Restaurant.

Description: The trail first skirts a service road and then wends its way uphill to a communications installation with large receiving dishes at the top of Bushytop Mountain. Continue straight to reach a junction at 0.2 mile with the trail to Millers Head to the left. Straight ahead, Bushytop Overlook gives a view of Kettle Canyon below and Skyland back to your right.

Take the turn left to continue on to Millers Head. You'll descend along the ridgeline with several switchbacks right and left. You'll zigzag down a rock outcrop at 0.7 mile and then wind your way up to a stone observation deck at the point of Millers Head at 0.8 mile. The view is more that 180 degrees of the Page Valley/Shenandoah Valley to the east with Massanutten Mountain in the distance.

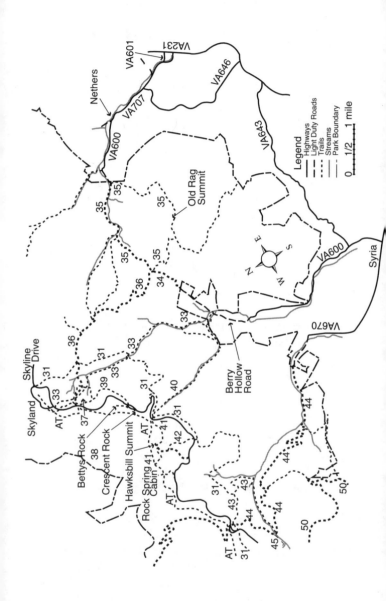

Map 7. Whiteoak Canyon to Rose River

98

33 Whiteoak Canyon Trail

5.3 miles one-way
(2.6 miles to Upper Falls one-way)
Moderate
Elevation loss: 2350 ft.
Cautions: Rocky, steep descent
Connections: Limberlost Trail, Old Rag Fire Road, Skyland-Big Meadows Horse Trail, Whiteoak Fire Road, Cedar Run Link Trail, Cedar Run Trail

Attractions: This trail gives access to the park's largest collection of waterfalls in one of the deepest canyons.

Trailhead: Just south of the southern entrance to Skyland, turn in the Whiteoak Canyon Parking on the east side of Skyline Drive at Mile 42.6.

Description: The trail enters the woods and descends. At 0.5 mile, you'll cross a branch of Whiteoak Run on a footbridge. Soon after, the trail crosses the Limberlost Trail and at 0.6 mile crosses Old Rag Fire Road. At 0.8 mile, you'll cross the other side of the Limberlost Trail and bear left along another branch of Whiteoak Run on your right. The trail crosses a large bridge over this branch of Whiteoak Run at 1.2 miles and then follows the main stem of Whiteoak Run downstream on your left.

As you descend into Whiteoak Canyon, the creek cascades into pools among large hemlocks. At 1.5 miles you'll descend more steeply. The trail passes through large blocks of stone and at 2.4 miles turns left to cross a bridge over Whiteoak Run. A makeshift path stays straight along the creek to connect with the Whiteoak Fire Road.

After crossing the bridge, turn right downstream. Soon on your right you'll see the ford across to the Whiteoak Fire Road. You'll pass hitching rails and then the Skyland-Big Meadows Horse Trail up to the left. At 2.5 miles a path on the right leads to a view above the upper Whiteoak Falls. At 2.6 miles another path leads out onto rocks for a bird's-eye view of the 86-foot

Upper Falls of Whiteoak Run

100

falls, the second highest in the park.

The trail then begins a steep descent of rock steps to a junction at 2.8 miles with a 100-yard side trail right to the base of the upper falls. Continuing, you'll step down cemented stone steps and stone slabs. At 2.9 miles the trail swings around a huge boulder above a cascade in the creek. The trail descends left and right to a view of another falls of Whiteoak Run at 3.1 miles. You'll continue to descend, reaching an overlook of a third falls at 3.2 miles. As you continue the descent, watch for large hemlocks and poplars. At 3.3 miles you'll pass a short falls.

You'll then reach an overlook of another falls at 3.4 miles. Descending past this falls, you'll see a path to the right that leads down to a pool in the creek. The trail switchbacks down through rocks and hydrangea to emerge at the last falls of Whiteoak Run at 4.0 miles. This is a double falls; you'll see the second below.

Once below the falls, the descent is not so steep. You'll rock-hop a side stream. Whiteoak Run descends in small cascades. The trail continues to descend amid blooming laurel in May and June. You'll pass a little pool below a cascade in the creek.

At 4.5 miles, you'll reach a junction with the Cedar Run Link Trail to the right. This trail links with the Cedar Run Trail for one of the best loop hikes in the park—across the link trail to the Cedar Run Trail; up Cedar Run to Hawksbill Gap on Skyline Drive at Mile 45.6 (Trail #40), north on the Skyland-Big Meadows Horse Trail and right on the Whiteoak Fire Road (Trail #31) to rejoin the Whiteoak Canyon Trail above the upper falls for a loop of 7.8 miles, plus 4.8 miles round-trip from the parking area. Take care on the Cedar Run Link Trail, which was severely eroded during a 1996 storm spawned by Hurricane Fran.

Continue your descent along Whiteoak Run, crossing the creek on a metal bridge and reaching a junction at 5.1 miles with the Cedar Run Trail, where you can also turn right to walk the Whiteoak/Cedar Run Loop. Bear left on the Whiteoak Canyon Trail and ford Cedar Run; a bridge here was damaged in the 1996 storm. You'll reach the upper end of the parking area for the lower trailhead at 5.3 miles. Walking through the parking area, you'll cross back over Cedar Run and pass through more parking to reach VA600 (Berry Hollow Road).

Lower Falls of Whiteoak Run

𝟥𝟦 Berry Hollow Fire Road

0.8 mile one-way
Easy
Elevation gain: 400 ft. (1700 ft. to Old Rag Summit)
Cautions: Uphill, rocky and rutted
Connections: Whiteoak Canyon Trail, Cedar Run Trail,
Old Rag Fire Road, Weakley Hollow Fire Road, Saddle Trail

Attractions: This road gives access to the lower end of the Whiteoak Canyon and Cedar Run Trails and the easiest access to the summit of Old Rag.

Trailhead: Exit the park at Thornton Gap and descend east on US211; turn south on US522 in Sperryville. In 0.6 mile turn right onto VA231. Turn right on VA643 at 11.0 miles. At 15.5 miles, you'll reach a junction with VA600. To the left, you can reach the community of Syria on VA670 (staying at Graves' Mountain Lodge near Syria, we had easy access up VA600 to this junction). Turn right up VA600 toward the park. At 19.3 miles, the road crosses Cedar Run and passes parking on the left for the lower end of Cedar Run and Whiteoak Canyon Trails. The road crosses Whiteoak Run. Continue up the narrow gravel road to its end at 20.2 miles. Berry Hollow Fire Road heads uphill to the right. You'll find a registration stand; the park now collects $3.00 for access to Old Rag on weekends and holidays from Memorial Day to the end of October; your park pass is good for this fee.

Description: The old road winds uphill to a junction at 0.8 mile where stood the post office/store for the community of Old Rag. Old Rag Fire Road heads west to Skyline Drive in 5.0 miles. Just up that road and right, the Weakley Hollow Fire Road leads down to trailhead parking for Old Rag on the north. The Saddle Trail turns right off Berry Hollow Fire Road, ascending to the summit of Old Rag in 2.0 miles for a total one-way hike of 2.8 miles— an easier hike to the summit than the Ridge Trail (Trail #35) and shorter than the Old Rag Fire Road from Skyline Drive.

㍟ Ridge Trail/ Saddle Trail/ Weakley Hollow Loop

7.1 miles
(Old Rag Summit 2.6 miles one-way)
Difficult
Elevation change: 2284 ft.
Cautions: Rock scramble, not recommended when rocks are wet; lots of people on weekends and holidays
Connections: Nicholson Hollow Trail, Old Rag Fire Road, Berry Hollow Fire Road, Robertson Mountain Trail, Corbin Hollow Trail

Attractions: This interesting hike takes you over the summit of Old Rag Mountain for panoramic views from the bare rock peak.

Trailhead: On the east side of the park at Sperryville, turn southeast on US522 for 0.6 mile to a right turn onto VA231. At 8.7 miles turn right onto VA601 and then at 9.1 miles turn right to continue on 601. The road bears left at 10.0 miles and becomes VA707. Stay left again at 11.7 miles as the road becomes VA600 in the community of Nethers. At 12.2 miles you'll reach lower parking for the trailhead; on busy weekends and holidays, parking is restricted to this lower lot, which will add 0.9 mile one-way to your hike. At 12.8 miles, you'll pass the end of the Nicholson Hollow Trail on the right. You'll reach the upper trailhead parking for Old Rag at 13.1 miles. The park now collects an access fee of $3.00 per person over 16 years old on weekends and holidays from Memorial Day to the end of October to discourage overuse of this area. Try going on a weekday when fewer people about.

Description: The Weakley Hollow Fire Road heading straight into the woods will be your return route. Take the Ridge Trail to the left to hike the loop clockwise. You'll ascend through hemlock on a broad path. The trail switchbacks up the slope of Old

Rocky summit of Old Rag

Rag—from a distance the bare granite on top makes the peak look ragged.

At 1.6 miles, you'll reach the bare rock and boulders that make up the top of the mountain. From here you'll make a long and difficult rock scramble up to the peak; keep an eye on the blue blazes to find your way. At 1.8 miles, you'll drop into a narrow lava dike where the softer rock has eroded from between granite walls; the trail turns left at the end of the dike. You'll then drop through a saddle and continue up the mountain.

The trail penetrates a rock squeeze and at 1.9 miles passes under a leaning boulder. Then turn right to the opening of another eroded dike and left inside. Out the other end, turn right. You'll have a brief reprieve before continuing the rock scramble. At one point, you must belly-up a boulder.

You'll reach the 3268-foot summit of Old Rag at 2.6 miles. A little farther you can scramble up rocks on the right to pause for a sweeping view; take care. At the summit, the Ridge Trail ends; but the path continues on, now as the Saddle Trail. You'll descend through boulders, switchbacks, and stone steps to reach Byrds Nest #1 Shelter at 3.1 miles. Built in 1961, the shelter is day-use only; there is no camping on Old Rag above 2800 ft. A fire road left heads southeast to end at the park boundary.

The trail bears right past the shelter, continuing to descend with switchbacks and through a rock passage. A large tree arched over the trail introduces an area of large trees. You'll reach the Old Rag Shelter at 4.2 miles, day-use only. The trail turns right on an old roadway. At 4.6 miles, you'll reach a junction of roads. To the left, the Berry Hollow Fire Road leads down to the park boundary and trailhead parking in 0.8 mile; this provides an easier route up Old Rag. Turn right on the Old Rag Fire Road and then right again on the Weakley Hollow Fire Road. Old Rag Road continues on to reach Skyline Drive in 5.0 miles.

On the Weakley Hollow Road at 5.7 miles you'll pass the Robertson Mountain Trail on the left and at 5.8 miles the Corbin Hollow Trail on the left. You'll cross Brokenback Run on a metal bridge and follow the creek downstream. At 7.0 miles, bear right to ford the creek to a series of metal and wooden bridges that take you over branches of the creek. You'll cross a side stream on a bridge and emerge back at trailhead parking at 7.1 miles.

Eroded dike on Old Rag

㉃ Old Rag Fire Road

5.0 miles one-way
(Summit of Old Rag 7.0 miles)
Moderate
Elevation loss: 1460 ft.
Cautions: None
Connections: Skyland-Big Meadows Horse Trail,
Limberlost Trail, Whiteoak Canyon Trail,
Corbin Mountain Trail, Corbin Hollow Trail,
Robertson Mountain Trail, Saddle Trail,
Weakley Hollow Fire Road, Berry Hollow Fire Road

Attractions: This old road passes through a forest of hemlocks called "The Limberlost" and provides access from Skyline Drive to Old Rag Mountain.

Trailhead: At Mile 43.0 turn in the Old Rag Fire Road on the east side of the Drive, there's no sign. You'll find a parking area that is also the trailhead for the Limberlost Trail on the left.

Description: As you head down the Old Rag Fire Road you'll pass the horse trail from the Skyland stables joining the road on the left. Soon after, the Whiteoak Canyon Trail for hikers crosses the road and you'll then enter The Limberlost, a forest of 270- to 370-year-old hemlocks. At 0.6 mile, you'll cross the lower portion of the Limberlost Trail.

You'll then descend to cross the upper part of Whiteoak Run. Soon after, you'll reach a fork. To the right a short path provides a turnaround area for guided, one-hour horse rides from the stables. Stay with the road to the left as it ascends.

At 1.1 miles, you'll reach a junction with the Skyland-Big Meadows Horse Trail turning off the road to the right. Just up the road, the Skyland-Big Meadows Horse Trail from the Skyland north entrance comes in on the left. Continue headed east on the Old Rag Fire Road.

The Corbin Mountain Trail leads left off the road at 1.9 miles up to a junction with the Indian Run Trail and then over Corbin

Mountain to the Nicholson Hollow Trail in 4.4 miles.

At 2.4 miles along the Old Rag Fire Road, the Corbin Hollow Trail leads left down the hollow of Brokenback Run to connect with the Weakley Hollow Fire Road in 2.0 miles. And at 2.5 miles, the Robertson Mountain Trail leads left over Robertson Mountain to connect with the Weakley Hollow Fire Road in 2.4 miles.

At 5.0 miles, the Old Rag Fire Road descends into the gap between the Blue Ridge to the west and Old Rag Mountain to the east. On ahead lies the Berry Hollow Fire Road that leads 0.8 mile down to a parking area at the end of vehicle access from the east. At the junction of the Old Rag and Berry Hollow Fire Roads, the Weakley Hollow Fire Road comes in on the left and, just beyond, the Saddle Trail heads left up to the summit of Old Rag Mountain in another 2.0 miles. The Weakley Hollow Fire Road and the Saddle Trail are part of a difficult loop hike across the summit of Old Rag (Trail #35).

37 Limberlost Loop

1.3 miles
Easy
Elevation change: Gently sloping
Cautions: No camping
Connections: Old Rag Fire Road,
Skyland-Big Meadows Horse Trail, Whiteoak Canyon Trail,
Crescent Trail

Attractions: The compact surface of the path and wooden walkways and bridges make this trail accessible for the physically challenged as it loops through a forest of large hemlocks.

Trailhead: At Mile 43.0 on Skyline Drive turn east onto the Old Rag Fire Road. In 0.1 mile, you'll find an open area and parking for the trailhead. (Refer to Map 6 for details.) This trail was damaged by a storm in 1996 but is scheduled to be reconstructed by Fall 1997.

Description: To the left, you'll see the sign for the trailhead where you'll begin the walk. To the right across Old Rag Fire Road, you'll see the return portion of the loop.

In 100 yards after beginning the trail, you'll cross the branch of the Skyland-Big Meadows Horse Trail that leads from the stables near the south entrance of Skyland to the Old Rag Fire Road. Continue straight on the Limberlost Trail. The trail passes through mountain laurel and then at 0.3 mile crosses the Whiteoak Canyon Trail where you'll see the first of several benches that sit along the trail approximately every 400 feet for rest stops.

The trail curves to the right as it begins the loop in a clockwise direction. At 0.5 mile you'll cross the Old Rag Fire Road and soon after again cross the Whiteoak Canyon Trail.

The Limberlost Trail wanders through the hemlock forest called "The Limberlost," the name taken by George F. Pollock from the Gene Stratton Porter novel *A Girl of the Limberlost*. The Limberlost, as Porter knew it, was a forested swamp in northeastern Indiana.

110

We walked the Limberlost Trail on a late afternoon with the 270- to 370-year-old trees shrouded in fog and mist. Deer stood, fearlessly watching us pass. Birds flew among the understory. A lone black bear climbed a tree to our left.

At 0.6 mile the trail crosses a bridge over a stream that is part of the headwaters of Whiteoak Run. Watch for huge hemlocks through this next section of trail. At 0.9 mile you'll reach a junction with the Crescent Rock Trail to the left that leads 1.1 miles to the Crescent Rock Overlook at Mile 44.4 on Skyline Drive. Stay straight to cross a long boardwalk over a low, swampy area where you may see the speckled alder, a large shrub that can get to twenty feet high with broadly elliptical to oval alternating leaves; the shrub is rare in Virginia. At 1.3 miles, you'll emerge to cross Old Rag Fire Road back to the parking area and the trailhead.

Skyline Drive: Continuing down Skyline Drive from Old Rag Fire Road, you'll pass through an old apple orchard, laden with blooms in early spring and fruit later on. At the Timber Hollow Overlook at Mile 43.3, you'll see Hawksbill Mountain to the left, the highest peak in the park, and Nakedtop Mountain. In the foreground to the left lies Timber Hollow, which is actually the upper end of Bruacker Hollow. The prominent peak to the right is Pollock Knob, named in 1951 in honor of George F. Pollock, the founder of Skyland Resort who helped lead the effort to establish Shenandoah National Park; Pollock died in 1949. By descending steps from this overlook into the clearing below, you can connect with the AT that runs below the overlook.

㊳ Crescent Rock & Bettys Rock

100 yards and 0.3 mile one-way
Moderate
Elevation gain: 100 ft. to Bettys Rock
Cautions: Steep drop-offs
Connections: Appalachian Trail

Attractions: These two rocks provide panoramic views to the west with only short walks.

Trailhead: Turn in the parking area for the Crescent Rock Overlook at Mile 44.4 where you'll have a view to the southwest of Hawksbill and Nakedtop Mountains.

Description: From the south end of the overlook parking, a path leads 100 yards to Crescent Rock, which provides a view west with the high Hawksbill Mountain and Nakedtop to the left and Timber/Bruacker Hollow below. Crescent Rock is a popular place for picnics and for viewing sunrises and sunsets.

From the north end of the parking area, walk up steps and take the path straight to get to Bettys Rock. A side trail to the left leads 150 yards down to connect with the AT, which passes below the Crescent Rock Overlook. Stay with the gravel path straight, and you'll ascend gradually 0.3 mile to Bettys Rock, another popular place for sunsets with virtually the same view as from Crescent Rock; but also to the right you'll see Millers Head, Bushytop, and Stony Man. Bettys Rock is likely named for Betty Sours, who once lived in the area.

Bettys Rock

㉟ Crescent Rock Trail

1.1 miles one-way
Moderate
Elevation loss: 320 ft.
Cautions: Heavily eroded
Connections: Limberlost Trail

Attractions: This trail leads to the Limberlost Trail along a path lined with ferns and frequent pinxter-flower blooming in spring.

Trailhead: From the northern end of the Crescent Rock Overlook parking area at Mile 44.4, cross Skyline Drive to the east side to pick up the Crescent Rock Trail.

Description: Head into the woods. You'll ascend at first and then, after a relatively level section, begin a gradual descent. This trail was heavily eroded by the 1996 storm; watch your footing.

At 1.0 mile, a path to the left ascends to an old housesite with a fence. Then at 1.1 miles, you'll reach a junction with the Limberlost Trail. To the left, you can cross a boardwalk and reach trailhead parking for the Limberlost Trail on the Old Rag Fire Road in 0.4 mile. To the right, you can reach the Whiteoak Canyon Trail and then the Old Rag Fire Road, also in 0.4 mile.

Skyline Drive: You'll pass the Whiteoak Fire Road on the east side of Skyline Drive at Mile 45.0 where there's room for a couple of cars to park. At 0.1 mile down this fire road you can connect with the Skyland-Big Meadows Horse Trail, which follows the fire road to the left to reach the upper falls of Whiteoak Canyon in 1.7 miles; this is the shortest access to the falls.

④⓪ Cedar Run Trail

3.1 miles one-way
Moderate
Elevation change: 2100 ft.
Cautions: Rocky footing, stinging nettle, steep descent,
eroded on the lower section
Connections: Skyland-Big Meadows Horse Trail,
Cedar Run Link Trail, Whiteoak Canyon Trail

Attractions: Cascading streams make this a grand hike through one of the deep canyons of the Blue Ridge.

Trailhead: At Mile 45.6, you'll reach Hawksbill Gap with parking on both sides of the Drive. For this hike, park in the small area on the east side of the Drive. The lower sections of this trail were seriously eroded in the storm of 1996; so use caution as you walk the trail.

Description: Take the path straight into the woods. You'll soon encounter a fork; the right fork is the Skyland-Big Meadows Horse Trail headed south toward Big Meadows. Stay to the left. You'll reach another fork with the horse trail turning left toward Skyland to the north. Keep straight to continue on the Cedar Run Trail.

You'll begin a steep, rocky descent along Cedar Run on your right. At 0.6 mile the trail turns right. You'll then pass a number of cascades in the creek and walk along a tall rock wall on the left as the trail continues down Cedar Run Canyon. At 1.1 miles watch for a broad rock beside a nice wading pool in the creek.

At 1.3 miles, the trail bears right to ford Cedar Run below a winding cascade. You'll then ascend from the creek and cross a small side stream. The trail then descends again as Cedar Run continues to cascade steeply down the canyon. After curving left and right, the trail switchbacks down to the creek at 1.6 miles where you'll see the water gliding down a smooth rock slide. Below is the top of 34-foot Cedar Run Falls. The trail descends steeply to the right to reach an unofficial side trail on the left at

1.7 miles that drops to the bottom of a sluice of water that is the lower part of the falls.

Continuing on the trail, you'll bear left down stone steps. The trail then drops into a forest of large poplars. At 2.2 miles, you'll pass another sluice in the creek as the trail continues steeply down to cross a small side stream. You'll pass another long cascade as you descend through large hemlocks. The trail turns down left, curves right, and turns down left again to ford Cedar Run below a 12-foot waterfall at 2.6 miles.

At 2.8 miles, you'll reach a junction with the Cedar Run Link Trail to the left. This trail links with the Whiteoak Canyon Trail for one of the best loop hikes in the park; take care on the Cedar Run Link Trail, which was washed out during the storm of 1996. On the link trail, you'll climb and circle the ridge separating Cedar Run Canyon from Whiteoak Canyon. You'll pass through a hemlock wood and curve up Whiteoak Canyon. In 0.8 mile, you'll ford Whiteoak Run and reach a junction with the Whiteoak Canyon Trail. To complete the loop, turn up Whiteoak Canyon to above the upper falls (Trail #33), and turn left on the Whiteoak Fire Road and then turn south on the Skyland-Big Meadows Horse Trail (Trail #31) to get back to Hawksbill Gap for a loop hike of 7.8 miles.

At the junction with the Cedar Run Link Trail to the left, stay straight as the Cedar Run Trail continues steeply down the canyon. You'll connect with the Whiteoak Canyon Trail at 3.0 miles where you can also turn up left to walk the Whiteoak/Cedar Run Loop. Bear right on the Whiteoak Canyon Trail and cross Cedar Run; a bridge here was damaged in the '96 storm, so if it has not been repaired or replaced, you must ford the creek.

You'll reach the upper end of the parking area for the trailhead off Berry Hollow Road in 3.1 miles. Walking through the parking area, you'll cross back over Cedar Run and pass through more parking to reach the road.

Lower step of Cedar Run Falls

41 Hawksbill/Salamander/ AT Loop

2.8 miles
(Hawksbill Summit 0.9 mile one-way)
Easy
Elevation change: 650 ft.
Cautions: Rocky path
Connections: Byrds Nest #2 Service Road,
Hawksbill Mountain Trail, Appalachian Trail

Attractions: This short hike leads to a grand view atop Hawksbill Mountain, the highest peak in Shenandoah National Park.

Trailhead: Begin at Hawksbill Gap parking on the west side of the Drive at Mile 45.6.

Description: The Hawksbill Trail heads straight into the woods to begin ascending as a steep, graveled path. As you climb into higher elevations, watch for balsam fir, mountain ash, and in June and July, the bell-shaped flowers of minnie bush.

At 0.8 mile, you'll reach a junction with the service road that leads from Skyline Drive at Mile 47.1 to Byrds Nest #2 shelter just to your right. Built in 1962, the shelter is for day-use only; there's no camping allowed on the summit of Hawksbill.

Turn right to pass in front of the shelter. On the other side you'll see a path to the right that passes behind the shelter to reconnect with the trail you came up. At 0.9 mile you'll reach the top of the 4050-foot peak of Hawksbill Mountain; a stone observation platform offers a 360-degree view of the Blue Ridge. To the north, look for Stony Man, and to the northeast, look for Old Rag.

Backtrack down past the shelter to the junction with the Hawksbill Trail at 1.0 mile. Then continue straight down the service road. At 1.1 miles you'll reach a junction with the Salamander Trail to the right. If you were to continue down the service road, you'd reach Skyline Drive in 0.8 mile, or in 0.1 mile you could

Byrds Nest #2

Southwest View from Hawksbill

turn left onto the Hawksbill Mountain Trail that leads toward the Upper Hawksbill Parking Area at Mile 46.7 on Skyline Drive. To make the loop hike described here, turn right on the Salamander Trail, recently renamed from the "Nakedtop" Trail.

You'll pass a rock outcrop with a view to the right while the rocky path bears left along the edge of the mountain. You'll pass a short connector path over to the service road, and then the trail makes a winding descent to a junction with the Appalachian Trail at 1.8 miles. To the left on the AT, you'd reach Fishers Gap in 2.2 miles. Turn right to complete the loop.

Along this section of the AT watch for speckled wood lily in May and June and, in summer in rocky areas, Allegheny stonecrop. The path is rough in places where it traverses talus slopes.

The trail descends into Hawksbill Gap past the parking area to a junction at 2.8 miles where the AT continues straight toward Skyland. The path to the left leads 100 yards down to a spring, while the path on the right leads 50 yards back up to the Hawksbill Gap parking area to complete the loop.

Skyline Drive: At Mile 45.6, Old Rag View Overlook on the east offers another look at Old Rag Mountain.

42 Hawksbill Mountain Trail

0.7 mile one-way
(Hawksbill Mountain Summit 1.0 mile one-way)
Moderate
Elevation gain: 400 ft.
Cautions: Steep ascent
Connections: Skyland-Big Meadows Horse Trail,
Byrds Nest #2 Service Road, Salamander Trail,
Hawksbill Trail

Attractions: This trail provides additional access to the summit of Hawksbill Mountain.

Trailhead: Begin at the Upper Hawksbill Parking Area on the west side of Skyline Drive at Mile 46.7. Across the road and to the south, you'll also find a short connector to the Skyland-Big Meadows Horse Trail.

Description: From the parking area, head straight into the woods on a graveled path that begins a steep ascent up Hawksbill Mountain. You'll pass benches on the left and the right and, at 0.4 mile, pass a large tablerock on the right.

After a level section of trail, you'll reach a junction at 0.7 mile with the Byrds Nest #2 Service Road. To the left you can descend 0.7 mile on the service road to reach Skyline Drive at Mile 47.1; there's very little parking at that location. Turn right to access the summit.

The fire road climbs steeply, entering the no-camping zone around the summit and passing through the standing skeletons of dead trees. You'll reach a junction at 0.8 mile with the Salamander Trail that leads left down to the AT.

Continue up the service road. At 0.9 mile you'll reach a junction with the Hawksbill Trail to the right and, just beyond, the Byrds Nest #2 Shelter. Watch for an abundance of sunflowers in summer. Continue straight in front of the shelter to reach the summit at 1.0 mile.

Skyline Drive: Continuing south on Skyline Drive, you
the service road on the west side at Mile 47.1 that ascen
Byrds Nest #2 Shelter.

You'll pass another service road on the west side at Mile
47.8 that leads to the PATC Rock Spring Cabin; the Rock Spring
Hut on the AT stands near the cabin. At Mile 48.1 at the Spitler
Knoll Overlook, a 50-yard path at the north end of the overlook
parking leads steeply down to the AT, where you can turn right
to walk to Rock Spring Cabin in 0.8 mile. From the overlook,
named for a family that had a farm nearby, you'll see Blackrock
Mountain to the left where the lodge and campground near Big
Meadows are located; to the right stands Nakedtop.

At Mile 49.0 at the Franklin Cliffs Overlook, named for
William B. Franklin, Union general in the Civil War, you can
see the town of Stanley below and the high peak of Blackrock
to your left.

Did 24 4/98+

3 Rose River Loop 4/00

Great
3.9 miles
Hiked.
se River Falls 1.2 miles one-way)
Moderate
Elevation change: 800 ft.
Cautions: Rocky path, stream crossings and ford
Connections: Appalachian Trail,
Skyland-Big Meadows Horse Trail, Rose River Fire Road,
Dark Hollow Falls Trail

Attractions: Along the Rose River and Hogcamp Branch, you'll pass numerous pools and cascades, including the double drop of Rose River Falls. Also a good walk for wildflowers in spring.

Trailhead: At Mile 49.4, Fishers Gap Overlook offers a view down Kite Hollow to the west. At the north end of the parking area, a road crosses Skyline Drive; this was the Gordonsville Turnpike, which was used during the Civil War by Stonewall Jackson and his troops to cross the mountains on the way east, following their successful Valley Campaign. On the west, the road is now called the "Redgate Fire Road," and on the east, the "Rose River Fire Road." You can access the AT down the Redgate Road or by a short path at the south end of the overlook. The Redgate Road descends the mountain on the west to emerge from the park as VA611. To walk the Rose River Loop, cross the Drive to the east and head down the Rose River Fire Road.

Description: Very soon after leaving the Drive, the trail turns left off the fire road to make a clockwise loop. This wide path to the left off the fire road is blazed yellow because it is also part of the Skyland-Big Meadows Horse Trail. At 0.1 mile, a post marks 9.5 miles for horse riders from Skyland. At 0.5 mile, you'll reach a junction with the horse trail turning off to the left. Continue straight on the Rose River Loop, blazed blue for hikers.

At 0.9 mile, the trail bends to the right where an abandoned path leads left. You'll descend through a hemlock grove to reach the Rose River tumbling into a rock-walled ravine. Bear right to

124

parallel the river downstream. At 1.2 miles, you'll reach the top of Rose River Falls. A steep path down to the base of the 30-foot drop gives access to the plunge pool, a good swimming hole.

Straight ahead, the trail turns up to the right. But also a makeshift path to the left weaves between the rocks and descends steeply to the river below the falls. Turning back left along the stream, you'll reach the plunge pool of a lower 30-foot falls where the water slides down a crack in the rock. Since the upper pool already had hikers in it, we decided to jump in here on a hot summer day and screamed as we hit the bone-chilling water.

Turning right above the upper falls, the trail ascends and then bears left to continue following the Rose River downstream. At 1.7 miles, the trail makes a sharp right to begin an ascent up Hogcamp Branch. A path to the left at the turn leads onto the point of land between Hogcamp Branch and the Rose River to an old housesite. Heading up Hogcamp Branch, you'll pass at 1.8 miles a concrete block that served as a base for machinery used in mining copper up the slope to your right in the early 1900s; the mine site was worked originally in 1845-50.

You'll rockhop a side stream and at 1.9 miles cross Hogcamp Branch. A metal bridge here was damaged by the 1996 storm; so you must ford the creek until the bridge can be repaired. Just on the other side, an unmaintained path leads left 0.3 mile up to the Rose River Fire Road; this path is not recommended. Stay with the trail, which ascends through rocks to continue upstream. You'll pass numerous mini-step cascades, water slides, and pools in this lovely stream. At 2.4 miles, watch for a 15-foot falls.

The trail leads up to a junction with the Rose River Fire Road at 2.9 miles. Turn right to cross Hogcamp Branch on a metal bridge. You'll then reach a junction with the Dark Hollow Falls Trail to the left; you can reach the bottom of Dark Hollow Falls on Hogcamp Branch in 0.2 mile up this trail.

Continue straight up the fire road to complete the loop. At 3.4 miles, a path to the left leads up to the Cave Cemetery. Just before returning to Skyline Drive, you'll pass the Skyland-Big Meadows Horse Trail turning off the road to the left, and then close the loop with the horse trail to the right. Up to the Drive at 3.9 miles, you'll cross the highway to return to the Fishers Gap Overlook Parking.

Rose River Falls

126

44 Rose River Fire Road

6.6 miles one-way
Easy
Elevation gain: 2000 ft.
Cautions: Rocky
Connections: Upper Dark Hollow Trail, Stony Mountain Trail,
Rose River Loop, Dark Hollow Falls Trail,
Skyland-Big Meadows Horse Trail

Attractions: This fire road gives access to the Rose River at its lower end for fishing and swimming and access to several trails.

Trailhead: The upper end of the Rose River Fire Road lies at Mile 49.4 at Fishers Gap and is part of the Rose River Loop (Trail #43). But you also have access from outside the park. Follow the directions in Trail #34 toward Berry Hollow. At the junction of VA643 and VA600 turn left, instead of right toward Berry Hollow. At 0.9 mile, you'll reach the community of Syria at a junction with VA670. You can also reach Syria along VA670 from VA231 on the east, passing through Criglersville. Continue west on 670. You'll pass the Graves' Mountain Lodge on the hill to the left; we stayed here when we hiked this region and had easy access to trails on this side of the park. At 1.4 miles from Syria, the road becomes gravel. You'll cross a bridge over the Rose River at 2.6 miles and reach parking at 3.2 miles.

Description: The Rose River Fire Road into the park was once the Gordonsville Turnpike; Gordonsville lies to the east. Officially, the road was called the "Blue Ridge Turnpike" when Paschal Graves was in charge of construction of the road on the east side of the mountain. When the road was completed in the 1850s, Graves opened an "ordinary," or inn, along the road. His great-great grandson, Jim Graves, and Jim's wife, Rachel, operate today's Graves' Mountain Lodge.

Head up the old road; you'll find the footing rocky. Where the road enters the park, you'll pass around a chain blocking vehicle access. The road is blazed yellow for horse use.

127

Rose River and Hogcamp Branch offer recreational fishing

At first, the Rose River lies far below on your right. But soon the road gets closer to the river and at 0.6 mile a path to the right leads down to the river's edge at a broad pool great for swimming or trout fishing. At 1.1 miles the road crosses a bridge over a side stream. Watch for another path right down to the river at 1.3 miles. Here the river drops through several pools. At this path, the road curves left away from the river.

At 1.4 miles, where the road curves right, the Upper Dark Hollow Trail leads to the left. On that horse trail you'd ascend Dark Hollow to emerge on a road at 0.7 mile; to the left, you would exit from the park to pass the PATC Meadows Cabin (for members only) and reach VA648. The Upper Dark Hollow Trail turns right on the road to its end and then continues as a trail through a section of the Rapidan Wildlife Management Area to connect in 2.0 miles with the Rapidan Fire Road. The Upper Dark Hollow Trail suffered damage in the '96 storm; check at the visitor center for whether it has been cleared and repaired.

The Rose River Fire Road continues up the mountain from the Upper Dark Hollow Trail. Watch for a large white pine and in summer wild raspberries along the road. At 4.0 miles, a post on the left marks an unmaintained path on the right that leads down to the Rose River Loop; not recommended.

Where the road curves right at 4.7 miles, you'll reach the Stony Mountain Trail on the left. This trail, which also suffered damage in the '96 storm, ascends the steep slope of Stony Mountain to emerge on the Rapidan Fire Road in 1.1 miles.

From the junction with the Stony Mountain Trail, the Rose River Fire Road continues up to a junction with the Rose River Loop just before the crossing of Hogcamp Branch on a metal bridge at 5.6 miles. On the other side, the Dark Hollow Falls Trail leads up to the left. Continuing, you'll pass the Cave Cemetery on the left and reach Skyline Drive at Fishers Gap at 6.6 miles. The Skyland-Big Meadows Horse Trail crosses the road just before the Drive. The horse trail to the north is the beginning of the Rose River Loop; to the south, the horse trail crosses the Drive at Mile 49.5.

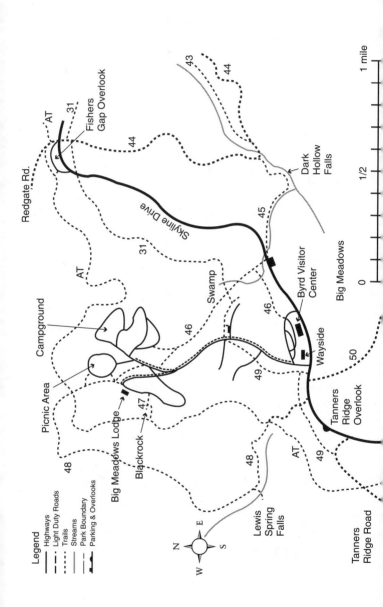

Map 8. Big Meadows Area

130

4️⃣5️⃣ Dark Hollow Falls Trail

0.8 mile one-way
Moderate
Elevation loss: 600 ft.
Cautions: Steep descent, crowded
Connections: Rose River Fire Road/
Rose River Loop

Attractions: This most popular trail in the park takes you by Dark Hollow Falls.

Trailhead: Begin at the Dark Hollow Falls Parking on the east side of Skyline Drive at Mile 50.7. At the far left of the parking area, take the paved path down beside the Drive. You'll also see a path to the left that crosses the Drive; this is a paved connector to the Story-of-the-Forest Nature Trail and the parking area at the Byrd Visitor Center.

Description: Down the Dark Hollow Falls Trail, you'll cross a culvert over the upper part of Hogcamp Branch, which drains the Big Meadows Swamp that's off the nature trail on the other side of the Drive. After the crossing of Hogcamp Branch, the path becomes a well-traveled, gravel path. In your descent, you'll pass rails to the right blocking shortcuts; please stay on the trail. You'll also pass several benches on your way down that you may need for short rests on the steep ascent back up.

The trail follows Hogcamp Branch downstream. The path swings right and then at 0.5 mile curves left at the confluence of a tributary of Hogcamp Branch which drains Big Meadow itself. You'll then follow along the combined waters of Hogcamp Branch as you continue the descent past small cascades.

At 0.6 mile you'll reach an overlook at the top of Dark Hollow Falls. Continue steeply down and curve right to reach the bottom for a better look at the 70-foot cascade. This is perhaps the most popular spot in the park—a waterfall only a short walk from the Drive—so you'll probably encounter many people along the trail and sitting at the falls.

Courtesy of Shenandoah National Park, photo by John Amberson

Dark Hollow Falls

From the base of the falls, the trail turns left to continue a steep descent along Hogcamp Branch with several cascades and small falls of water. You'll make a final descent with switch-backs to emerge on the Rose River Fire Road and the Rose River Loop at 0.8 mile.

Skyline Drive: At Mile 51.0 you'll reach Big Meadows, which lies on the east. You can turn right into the north entrance to the Big Meadows services complex. Here you'll find parking for the Harry F. Byrd Sr. Visitor Center, named for the Virginia Governor, and later Senator, who supported the establishment of the park and appointed the Virginia Conservation and Development Commission, which purchased the land for the park. The visitor center has an outside balcony and large windows overlooking Big Meadows. Perhaps first cleared by native Americans and later enlarged by settlers for cattle grazing, Big Meadows was once much larger, the forest now having reclaimed much of the open area. The park staff maintains Big Meadows at its current size as a shrub/meadows community. The dedication of the park by President Roosevelt in 1936 took place at Big Meadows.

46 Story-of-the-Forest Nature Trail Loop

1.8 miles
Easy
Elevation change: 150 ft.
Cautions: Horse crossing
Connections: Dark Hollow Falls Trail

Attractions: This easy loop hike introduces you to the Blue Ridge forest and the unique, high-elevation Big Meadows Swamp.

Trailhead: The nature trail begins to the right across from the Byrd Visitor Center parking area after you turn in the north entrance to the Big Meadows complex off Skyline Drive at Mile

51.0. You may also access the trail from the campground and by a short walk from the Big Meadows Lodge.

Description: You'll see the beginning of the nature trail at the edge of the woods across the road from the parking area. This is a self-guiding trail with interpretive signs. When you begin the trail, stay to the right on the paved path; straight ahead is access to a maintenance area.

You'll cross a stone bridge over the streambed of Hogcamp Branch at 0.2 mile and then reach a junction. To the right, the path emerges on Skyline Drive across from the Dark Hollow Falls Parking Area at mile 50.7. Turn left to continue on the nature trail, which is no longer paved from this point on. You'll cross back over the streambed on a metal bridge at 0.4 mile and reach an intersection with the Skyland-Big Meadows Horse Trail, which from the right has traveled all the way from Skyland and to the left leads to a parking area and a junction with the Tanners Ridge Horse Trail.

Stay straight on the nature trail and in 150 yards you'll see Big Meadows Swamp to the right. You can see where Hogcamp Branch emerges from the swamp. There are abundant wildflowers blooming in spring. Please observe from the edge of the swamp, and do not enter; foot traffic will cause soil compaction and vegetation damage in this ecologically fragile area.

Continue past the Big Meadows Swamp. You'll reach a left turn at 0.8 mile, where a path straight leads to the campground. Turning left, you'll come out to the campground road and connect with the paved trail that parallels the road between the campground/picnic area and the Big Meadows Wayside near the visitor center; just to the left a paved path also leads down from the Big Meadows Lodge. This paved path is open to bicycles. Turning left on the paved path you'll reach the wayside at 1.7 miles and walk through the parking area for the Byrd Visitor Center to your starting point at 1.8 miles.

47 Blackrock Summit

150 yards one-way
Easy
Elevation gain: 100 ft.
Cautions: Rock bluff
Connections: Appalachian Trail

Attractions: You'll have a great view west from the summit of Blackrock.

Trailhead: At Mile 51.2, turn in the south entrance to the Big Meadows complex. You'll pass the service center and the turn to the wayside and visitor center; keep going straight. Where the road forks to the right to the campground, stay to the left to get to the Big Meadows Lodge, operated by ARAMARK Virginia Sky-Line Company. Enter the parking area to the left of the lodge and look for signs where the trail begins near the end of the parking area.

Description: Take the paved path from the trailhead sign through the cabin area and then up the unpaved path. The ascent is somewhat rocky.

Near the summit you'll pass a communication installation on the left and then reach a trail to the left that leads down to a junction with the service road for the installation. At that junction, you can turn right to connect with the AT in 0.2 mile.

From the trail to the left, continue straight to a rock outcrop at the summit of Blackrock, at 3721 feet the fourth highest peak in the park. The view west makes a great sunset spot for those staying at the Big Meadows Lodge and a nice stroll after dinner at the lodge restaurant.

4⑧ Lewis Spring Falls Loop

3.0 miles
(Lewis Spring Falls 1.3 miles one-way)
Moderate
Elevation change: 800 ft.
Cautions: Rocky and steep in places
Connections: AT, Lewis Spring Service Road

Attractions: This loop swings by Lewis Spring Falls, an 81-foot cascading waterfall.

Trailhead: From the Big Meadows Lodge, walk to the north and look for a paved path leading into the woods at a sign that says "Big Meadows Lodge." The continuation of the paved walkway to the right leads back along the road to the Big Meadows Wayside and Skyline Drive.

Description: In a short distance down the trail, you'll reach a junction; the trail straight leads to the picnic area where you may also begin this hike. The trail right leads out to the campground road. Turn left to head for Lewis Falls. You'll see the amphitheater on the right as you walk down the trail, where you may also begin this hike; the amphitheater is accessed from the picnic area.

The trail intersects the AT at 0.1 mile. You'll complete this loop along the AT from the left. To the right, the AT leads to the Big Meadows Campground in 0.5 mile and Fishers Gap in 1.6 miles. Follow the blue-blazed Lewis Falls Trail straight ahead.

You'll descend from the AT, at times steeply, with flat rocks that you must walk across. At 0.6 mile you'll reach a rock bluff on the left. The trail traverses a more open area at 1.1 miles that affords views into the valley. You'll step up rocks several times and then pass over a rise at 1.2 miles. Watch for a boulder sitting atop another boulder on the right.

At 1.3 miles, you'll reach a 250-foot side trail to the right that leads to Lewis Spring Falls. Turn on the side path and you'll soon reach an overlook that gives a grand view of the valley.

From this overlook, another side trail to the right leads down to the foot of the waterfall, but the way is very steep and rocky and not recommended. Stay to the left, and the trail soon crosses the stream above the waterfall over rocks cemented together. Keep going up to a railing that takes you around to the observation point above Lewis Spring Falls, 81 feet high. This is one of the most picturesque waterfalls in the park, cascading into a steep gorge.

Back at the main trail, continue straight as the trail ascends from the waterfall side path. The trail is rocky along this section. You'll soon cross a stream where it runs under the trail in a culvert. You'll then follow a rock bluff on the left.

The trail meanders through a series of curves and switchbacks as it ascends toward the ridge line. At 1.7 miles, turn right where an abandoned section of trail leads straight. You'll pass a side path to the right that leads to an open level area. At 1.9 miles the trail reaches a junction with an old road that leads to the left. Turn right on the old roadbed to continue.

Here the way is graveled. You'll pass the pumping station for the Big Meadows area water supply on the left, a bermed structure with a locked door. You'll then pass a side path that leads to Lewis Spring, the source of the stream that forms Lewis Spring Falls. Then at 2.0 miles you'll ascend to a crossing of the AT. Straight ahead, you can walk the Lewis Spring Service Road 0.2 mile out to Skyline Drive at Mile 51.4. Right, the AT crosses Tanners Ridge Road in 0.6 mile and then crosses Skyline Drive at Milam Gap in 1.7 miles. Turn left.

Along the AT, you'll pass under the powerlines leading down to the pumping station you passed earlier. The trail ascends, rocky in places; you'll cross an old roadbed, now faint. At 2.4 miles, you'll reach a side path to the right that leads 0.2 mile up to the summit of Blackrock; from there it is a short walk down the other side to the parking lot for the lodge. But continue straight to complete the loop.

The AT passes below Blackrock and then behind the lodge, which you can see through the trees. You'll reach the junction with the Lewis Falls Trail at 2.9 miles. Turn right to get back to the trailhead and Big Meadows Lodge.

4️⃣9️⃣ Tanners Ridge Horse Trail

1.1 miles one-way
Easy
Elevation change: 100 ft.
Cautions: Can get overgrown
Connections: Skyland-Big Meadows Horse Trail,
Rapidan Fire Road, Tanners Ridge Road, Appalachian Trail

Attractions: This horse trail provides for a short warm-up ride and also an isolated walk for hikers and serves as access to the Rapidan and Tanners Ridge Roads.

Trailhead: At Mile 51.2, turn in the south entrance of the Big Meadows complex and head straight toward the lodge. You'll pass the service center and the turn to the wayside and visitor center and keep going straight. You'll then pass on the left a road into the waste water treatment plant and, at the next road, turn right toward the ranger maintenance area and pull in the parking area on the left that's also a RV/ trailer service area.

Description: At the far right side of the parking area, follow a service road into the woods. Soon you'll encounter a horse trail crossing the service road. To the right the trail becomes the Skyland-Big Meadows Horse Trail that leads 11.3 miles north to Skyland. Turn left here to ride the Tanners Ridge Horse Trail.

At 0.1 mile you'll cross the main road leading to the lodge and bear left into the woods away from a side road leading into a residence area. The trail crosses the paved road that leads to a wastewater treatment plant at 0.4 mile. You'll descend back into the woods where you'll see to the right an overgrown roadway that leads to the treatment plant. Just beyond is the junction of a return loop of the trail; it's not easy to spot so you may pass right by it. This return portion of the loop was not maintained when we were last there, and so we describe only the connection to Tanners Ridge Road.

This stretch of woods is a favorite deer haunt, so you'll see several standing in the woods or on the trail watching you. At

0.6 mile, you'll pass a path to the left that leads up to hitching rails and picnic tables. You can leave horses here to walk up to the wayside and visitor center.

Continuing straight, you'll reach boulders in the trail; passing through these boulders, you would emerge on Skyline Drive across from the Rapidan Fire Road. To continue the Tanners Ridge Horse Trail, turn to the right just before the boulders. At 0.8 mile, you'll reach a junction where the old loop comes together in the middle; stay to the left and you'll soon cross the Lewis Spring Service Road, which leads down from Skyline Drive to Lewis Falls.

Back into the woods after crossing the Lewis Spring Service Road, you'll pass through an overgrown area and emerge on Tanners Ridge Road at 1.1 miles. To the right the road heads down the mountain to emerge from the park and connect with VA682 in 1.2 miles; just down the road the AT crosses near the large Thomas/Meadows Cemetery, still used. To the left, the road leads up to Skyline Drive in 0.2 mile at Mile 51.6. Although this road is gated at both ends, you may encounter vehicles along here because the road is used by park employees who live in the valley.

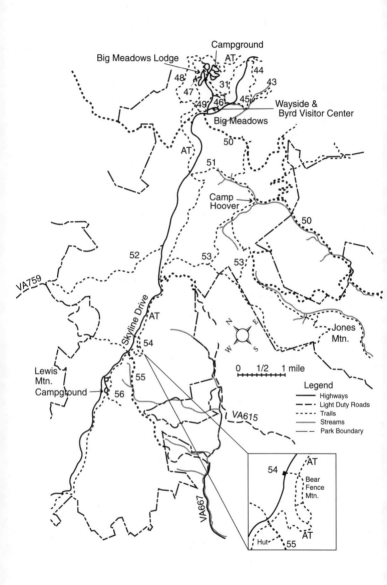

Map 9. Big Meadows to Lewis Mountain

5️⃣0️⃣ Rapidan Fire Road

10 miles one-way
Elevation loss: 2500 ft.
Moderate
Cautions: Rocky
Connections: Mill Prong Horse Trail, Stony Mountain Trail,
Upper Dark Hollow Trail, Camp Hoover

Attractions: This road offers a brief mountain bike ride and horse access to Camp Hoover.

Trailhead: At Mile 51.3, just past the Big Meadows South Entrance, turn in the Rapidan Fire Road on the east side of Skyline Drive. There's ample parking. The road is open to horses and, for the first mile, bicycles; this is the only trail section in the park open to bikes other than the paved trail from the Big Meadows lodge/campground to the Byrd Visitor Center.

Description: Proceed up the Rapidan Fire Road. The road circles the south end of Big Meadows and enters the woods at 0.6 mile. This is a popular walk for viewing the meadows and the abundant wildlife you'll see there at the end of the day. We have seen numerous deer and occasional black bear.

A side road to the left at 1.0 mile leads to a stone dumping area. At another road to the left at 1.1 miles, bikes must turn around because they are not allowed farther down the road. At 1.2 miles, the Mill Prong Horse Trail turns off to the right to lead down toward Camp Hoover; this trail is very rocky and eroded.

Continue down the road, which begins a descent of the mountain. At 3.0 miles, the Stony Mountain Trail leads to the left 1.1 miles to connect with the Rose River Fire Road. At 4.0 miles, the Upper Dark Hollow Trail also leads to the left to connect with the Rose River Fire Road in 2.0 miles.

At 5.9 miles, you'll reach a junction with a road to the right that leads half a mile to Camp Hoover, a fishing retreat established in 1929 by Pres. Herbert Hoover in a hemlock glade at the confluence of Laurel Prong and Mill Prong. These streams form

141

President's Cabin at Camp Hoover

the Rapidan River; originally pronounced "Rapid Anne," the river was named by colonial Governor Alexander Spotswood for Britain's Queen Anne. Pres. Hoover donated "Camp Rapidan," consisting of 13 structures, to the national park, and it became known as "Camp Hoover." Only three structures remain, including the President's Cabin, which is still available to the current President and Vice-President and other government officials.

On the Rapidan Fire Road, you can continue down the mountain past the turnoff for Camp Hoover. This was once the Criglersville Road and would have been the route used by Pres. Hoover to enter the area. At 6.3 miles, the road is gated where it enters a section of the Rapidan Wildlife Management Area. Before emerging from the wildlife management area, the road crosses the Rapidan; a bridge here was damaged by flood waters, and so you must ford the river until the bridge is repaired. At 8.0 miles, near the east boundary of the WMA, the Fork Mountain Road leads southwest to a radio tower. The Rapidan Fire Road continues straight along the river through another section of the park.

At 9.3 miles, you'll reach a fork with the Lower Rapidan Fire Road to the right leading southeast 1.7 miles to emerge from the park as VA662 and head toward Graves Mill; this lower portion of the fire road was destroyed by flooding the summer of 1995 and so for now is impassable. The left fork climbs from the river to a junction on Chapman Mountain where the Blakey Ridge Fire Road leads to the right to a lookout tower outside the park. The Chapman Mountain Road continues straight to emerge from the park at 10.5 miles as VA649, the Rapidan-Criglersville Road.

Skyline Drive: At Mile 51.4 the Lewis Spring Service Road on the west leads 0.2 mile down to connect with the Lewis Spring Falls Trail for the shortest access to Lewis Spring Falls, 0.9 mile. There's parking beside the service road. The Tanners Ridge Overlook at Mile 51.5 offers a view west with Tanners Ridge in the foreground, descending from the left, and the town of Stanley to the far right. At Mile 51.6 the Tanners Ridge Road heads down the mountain for access to the Tanners Ridge Horse Trail; where the AT crosses the road, 0.3 mile down from Skyline Drive, lies the Thomas/Meadows Cemetery, still maintained and used.

5️⃣1️⃣ Mill Prong Trail

1.8 miles one-way
(Big Rock Falls 1.5 miles one-way
Moderate
Elevation loss: 800 ft.
Cautions: Creek fords
Connections: AT, Mill Prong Horse Trail, Laurel Prong Trail

Attractions: The trail descends along Mill Prong past Big Rock Falls for the shortest access to Camp Hoover; a good walk for wildflowers in spring.

Trailhead: In Milam Gap, at Mile 52.8, turn in the parking area on the west. Notice the apple trees here; the apples of Joseph Milam were well known for keeping well through the winter and making fine brandy.

Description: To the left of the parking area you can access the AT. Turn left on the trail to cross Skyline Drive and at 0.1 mile reach a junction with the Mill Prong Trail on the left. If you were to continue straight on the AT you would reach the summit of Hazeltop Mountain in 1.9 miles, at 3812 feet the third highest peak in the park.

Turn left on the Mill Prong Trail, passing through the old Milam apple orchard on a wide path. At 0.4 mile you'll begin a descent into the hollow of Mill Prong. The trail turns left at 0.6 mile where the path straight has been abandoned. Soon after, you'll descend to a ford of Mill Prong. You'll walk up from the creek and then descend again to rockhop a side stream at 1.0 mile and reach a junction with the Mill Prong Horse Trail that leads left 1.0 mile up to the Rapidan Fire Road and provides horse access from Big Meadows. Bear right with the hiking and horse trails now coinciding down to Camp Hoover.

The trail bears left to once more parallel the cascading Mill Prong. You'll begin a steeper descent at 1.4 miles with switchbacks right and left and descend to Big Rock Falls on Mill Prong at 1.5 miles, a short cascade. You'll ford the creek below the falls

Big Rock Falls

and then turn right uphill, instead of staying straight along the creek.

Soon you'll be descending along the creek again through a hemlock forest to emerge on the Camp Hoover Road at 1.8 miles. The camp lies across the road. You are free to explore the compound that includes three of the original cabins, including the President's Cabin, but stay at a distance if the cabins are occupied. The camp sits above the confluence of Mill Prong with Laurel Prong; the two create the Rapidan River.

To first get an orientation, turn right on the road 100 yards to a path to the left that takes you by a display board that shows a map of the compound. To the right, the Laurel Prong Trail bears left off the road to head north.

Ahead, you'll see the President's Cabin, and to the right, the Prime Minister's Cabin, named for Britain's Prime Minister, Ramsay McDonald, who came to Camp Hoover to confer with the U.S. President on limiting the building of naval warships. To the far left of the compound, you'll find the Creel Cabin. An outdoor fireplace and a stone fountain still stand on the grounds. The other structures were dismantled because of a lack of funds to renovate and maintain them. During the years President Hoover used the camp, a marine camp housed troops to the east and a cabinet members camp was located farther down the Rapidan.

Beside the Prime Minister's Cabin, the President's Walk/ Fisherman's Loop leads up to Hemlock Run, a manmade run that once diverted water from Laurel Prong. The trail continues up the run to Laurel Prong where the small Laurel Dam controlled the water in Hemlock Run. The Fisherman's Loop continues up Laurel Prong. A profusion of wildflowers covers the ground in spring, some planted during the time the Hoovers occupied the camp; landscaping the area kept Mrs. Hoover busy while the President was fly-fishing. The trail eventually curves right and ascends to a junction with the Laurel Prong Trail; turn right to complete the one-mile loop back to Camp Hoover.

Skyline Drive: The Naked Creek Overlook at Mile 53.2 offers a view down the hollow of Naked Creek.

52 Powell Mountain Trail

3.6 miles one-way
(Summit of Powell Mountain 2.0 miles one-way)
Moderate
Elevation loss: 2000 ft.
(Elevation change to Powell Mountain Summit: 500 ft.
Cautions: Can get overgrown, some erosion
Connections: None

Attractions: A pleasant walk through wildflowers in late summer leads over the summit of Powell Mountain.

Trailhead: At Mile 54.4, turn in the Hazeltop Ridge Overlook on the west side of Skyline Drive. The long ridge running across the view in front of you is in fact Long Ridge. Powell Mountain stands to the left. You'll see a gap in the rock wall at the overlook that is the beginning of the Powell Mountain Trail.

Description: Walk through the gap and bear left across the open area below the overlook. In summer you'll see many spotted starthistle with purple-pink flowers, a non-native plant that grows in open areas. At 0.1 mile you'll enter the woods.

The trail bears right in a moderately steep descent that winds through the forest. At 0.6 mile, watch for the trail to jog right as you drop into a saddle between the main Blue Ridge and Powell Mountain. This is a cool pleasant walk through stands of boneset blossoming white in late summer. The trail heads up the flank of Powell Mountain to reach the ridgeline and bear left to top the first peak at 0.9 mile. The trail then descends the steep, rocky west slope. Keep an eye on the blazes to stay on the path.

The trail curves right through a wash and drops into another sag at 1.8 miles among tall poplars. You'll ascend over the summit of Powell Mountain at 2.0 miles; there are no views. The trail then begins a long winding descent of the southwest slope, emerging from the park and connecting with VA759 at 3.6 miles. Access here is questionable because of major flooding in 1996.

53 Laurel Prong/Fork Mountain/Jones Mountain/Cat Knob Loop

7.1 miles

Moderate

Elevation change: 1000 ft.

Cautions: Steep ascent and descent, creek ford, trail erosion

Connections: AT, Camp Hoover, Fork Mountain Road

Attractions: This loop provides for an isolated hike through forests of the Blue Ridge and introduces you to backcountry trails.

Trailhead: You'll find parking on the east side of the road at Bootens Gap on Skyline Drive at Mile 55.1. The Fairfax Line marking the southwest boundary of the lands of Lord Fairfax passed through Bootens Gap.

Description: A few paces down the Conway River Fire Road that heads straight into the woods, you'll turn left on the Appalachian Trail. The fire road continues southeast to leave the park in 1.4 miles and pass through a section of the Rapidan Wildlife Management Area and become VA615 leading toward the Graves Mill community. Francis Conway settled the area in the early 1700s.

At the junction with the AT, it's 11.6 miles south to Swift Run Gap. Turn left to head north on the AT. You'll make an ascent to a junction at 0.5 mile with the Laurel Prong Trail where you'll turn right. The AT continues north, in 0.5 mile crossing over Hazeltop; the AT then continues on another 1.9 miles to Milam Gap.

The Laurel Prong Trail moves down and up along the slope of the mountain to descend at 1.4 miles to a level area. The trail then drops off again to descend to Laurel Gap at 1.5 miles. Here you'll encounter the loop, with the Cat Knob Trail straight ahead, which will be your return route. Turn left here to stay on the Laurel Prong Trail.

148

The trail descends through an area called "The Laurels" for the profusion of mountain laurel. At 1.7 miles you'll pass a cut log on the left that makes a nice bench for lunch. The trail then descends through a hemlock woods; grouse burst from cover as we walked along this beautiful trail. Watch for a large hemlock to the right at 2.0 miles. You'll pass through a bottomland of ferns and then a large hemlock on the left.

The trail crosses several shallow side streams that feed the Laurel Prong to your right. Through this lowland watch for stacks of rocks left from when the area was settled. At 2.4 miles, you'll step over a stream flowing from a spring to the left of the trail.

At 2.8 miles, you'll reach a junction with the Fork Mountain Trail to the right. The Laurel Prong Trail continues straight here as a horse trail to reach Camp Hoover in another 0.6 mile. Turn right on the Fork Mountain Trail, a horse trail, to continue the loop. Downed trees from the '96 storm may make the trail impassable to horses; check with the visitor center for the state of repair.

You'll cross the small stream from above and then ford Laurel Prong at 2.9 miles. Following an old roadbed, the trail makes a steep and nearly continuous ascent up Fork Mountain to reach a junction at 4.1 miles with the Jones Mountain Trail to the right. This area is called "The Sag" because its the gap between Fork Mountain and Jones Mountain that separates the Staunton River watershed from the Laurel Prong drainage. Just ahead you can walk out to the Fork Mountain Road. To the left, the road leads up to an FAA radio tower; the summit also served as a signal point for both armies in the Civil War. Pres. Hoover had a lookout tower at the summit while he occupied his camp on the Rapidan. To the right, the road leads east and then north to enter the Rapidan Wildlife Management Area and connect with the Rapidan Fire Road, passing the Staunton River Trail along the way, which heads east to pass Jones Mountain and connect with the Rapidan Fire Road farther east. The flood of 1995 damaged the Staunton River Trail, washing away most of it from Jones Mountain east. On Jones Mountain stands the Jones Mountain Cabin, originally built by Albert Nichols in 1855 and restored by the PATC; the mountain bears the name of David Jones, who lived in the area in the 1740s. The Staunton River Valley includes 1000 acres of old-growth forest; only dead standing chestnut was taken in 1938 to build the cabins and lodge at Big Meadows.

Horse riders can use the Fork Mountain and Rapidan Roads along with the Fork Mountain Trail, once it's cleared, and sections of the Laurel Prong and Mill Prong Trails to make a circuit that includes a ride by Camp Hoover.

At the junction with the Jones Mountain Trail, turn right to head south, now back on a hiking trail. This trail can get overgrown in summer, but it had been recently cleared when we were last there. Watch for large stands of blue cohosh in summer with its blue berries and tall ferns scattered among mountain laurel. The trail mostly ascends, finally climbing steeply to a junction near the top of Cat Knob at 5.1 miles. The Jones Mountain Trail continues to the left, heading east to pass Bear Church Rock on Jones Mountain and connect with the Staunton River Trail. The Jones Mountain Trail was severely damaged by the '96 storm; check at the visitor center for the state of repair.

Turn right at this junction on the Cat Knob Trail. You'll ascend over Cat Knob and make a steep descent to Laurel Gap at 5.6 miles and a junction with the Laurel Prong Trail to close the loop. Continue straight on the Laurel Prong Trail to ascend to the AT and turn left to get back to Bootens Gap for a total of 7.1 miles.

Skyline Drive: At Mile 55.6 at The Point Overlook, look to the far right to see Hazeltop. You can take a path straight out from the overlook 100 yards to a rock outcrop offering a view west that is one of the best in the park, with ridge after ridge stretching into the distance; but the last time we were there the path was quite overgrown.

54 Bearfence Mountain Loop

1.2 miles
(Bearfence Mountain Summit 0.3 mile one-way)
Difficult
Elevation change: 300 ft.
Cautions: Steep drop-offs, rock scramble
Connections: Appalachian Trail

Attractions: This short hike offers a grand view from the top of Bearfence Mountain.

Trailhead: At mile 56.4 along Skyline Drive, you'll find parking for Bearfence Mountain on the west side of the road. To get to the trail, you must cross the Drive to the east side, where you'll see a sign indicating the Bearfence Rocks in 300 yards.

Description: The trail ascends from the Drive into a hardwood forest with ferns carpeting the forest floor. At several places along this trail and many other places in the park in summer, you'll find large patches of spotted jewelweed blooming orange. These flowers belong to the touch-me-not family, so named because in late summer when you touch the mature seed pods they pop open, throwing out their seeds.

In 100 yards, the trail crosses the Appalachian Trail, which to the right will be used to complete the loop. To the left, the AT leads north 1.4 miles to Bootens Gap and the Conway River Fire Road.

Continue straight on the Bearfence Mountain Loop. The trail curves left at a large rock, and then at 0.1 mile you'll begin ascending through rocks. At 300 yards you'll reach two outcroppings that are the first of the Bearfence Rocks along the ridge of Bearfence Mountain. These rocks appear to form a fence along the top of the mountain.

You'll descend and turn to the right to pass over another outcrop. You'll see to the left where people have tried to bushwhack around, but the trail actually goes right up over the rocks.

The trail drops to the ground again, and you'll pass more

outcroppings until at 0.3 mile you'll climb up to the summit of Bearfence Mountain. Halfway, you'll see a double blaze indicating a turn up through the rocks to the top. Steep drop-offs plunge down to your right; be careful and do not attempt this climb when the rocks are wet and slippery.

From the summit you'll have a 360-degree view of the surrounding mountains and valleys. To the southwest, you'll see a portion of Skyline Drive and to the west across the Shenandoah Valley, Massanutten Mountain. To the east, you'll see the Conway River Valley with Jones and Bluff Mountains beyond.

The trail from the summit continues south along the ridgeline. You'll descend and drop off to the right to continue along the trail. At 0.4 mile, you'll reach a junction with a short connector to the right that leads less than 100 yards to the AT. You can return along this connector if you want to shorten your loop by 0.3 mile.

Continuing past this junction, you'll ascend to a viewpoint to the west before the trail cuts across the ridgeline and then descends to a junction with the AT at 0.5 mile. To the left, the AT leads 0.6 mile to the Slaughter Fire Road.

Turn right on the AT to complete the loop. You'll now be following white blazes. The trail descends gradually until at 0.7 mile you'll reach a junction with the other end of the short connector you passed earlier. Continue straight on the AT, and at 1.1 miles you'll return to the junction near the beginning where the Bearfence Mountain Loop crossed the AT. Turn left to cross Skyline Drive and reach the parking area.

Bearfence Rocks

55 Slaughter Fire Road

3.8 miles one-way
Moderate
Elevation loss: 1700 ft.
Cautions: Can be overgrown, creek crossing
Connections: Appalachian Trail, Meadow School Trail

Attractions: You'll enjoy an isolated walk down an old fire road along Devils Ditch.

Trailhead: At Mile 56.8 on Skyline Drive, turn east onto the Slaughter Fire Road. You'll pass the AT crossing and find parking 100 yards from the Drive. North on the AT it's 7.8 miles to Big Meadows, and to the south it's 9.3 miles to Swift Run Gap. Also, you can walk back up the road to cross Skyline Drive to the Meadow School Trail that follows an old road down the mountain on the west to emerge from the park in 1.4 miles as VA759.

Description: Head down the Slaughter Fire Road. On the day we walked the trail the old roadbed had been mowed, which made for a pleasant stroll through isolated backcountry. In June you'll see plenty of blooming mountain laurel. At 0.2 mile, you'll reach another roadway to the right that leads 0.1 mile to the Bearfence Mountain Hut, where you can camp if you're hiking the AT. Continue straight on the Slaughter Road amid tall oaks. There was a good mast crop when we passed through; acorns crunched and popped underfoot and bounced off our heads.

A tall hemlock on the right at 0.7 mile sits on the edge of Devils Ditch, a tributary of the Conway River. The road descends to a crossing of the stream at 0.9 mile. Recent floods had washed away a culvert and the road, so we had to rockhop the stream at low water.

The road follows Devils Ditch downstream as it grows ever deeper. You'll eventually skirt a segment of the Rapidan Wildlife Management Area and emerge from the park to connect with VA667 at the Conway River at 3.8 miles.

56 Lewis Mountain Trail

0.5 miles one-way
Easy, then difficult
Elevation gain: 160 ft.
Cautions: Overgrown beyond the summit
Connections: Appalachian Trail

Attractions: If you're camping at Lewis Mountain, this trail makes a pleasant walk before you settle in for the night.

Trailhead: At Mile 57.5, turn in the Lewis Mountain complex. Stay right past the picnic area to the left. You'll pass cabins and the camp store, operated by the concessionaire. After you get your campsite or cabin, walk to the far left corner of the campground to site #16; you'll see the concrete post marking the beginning of the Lewis Mountain Trail.

Description: Head straight into the woods from the edge of the campground. In 50 yards, you'll cross the AT. If you are not staying at Lewis Mountain, you can enter the picnic area and, at about three-fourths of the way around the one-way loop, access the AT by a 120-yard path to the right and then turn south on the AT to this junction with the Lewis Mountain Trail. Or you can park at the camp store and walk the road into the campground.

You'll pass an elevation marker in the middle of the trail. Stay left at a path to the right at 0.2 mile. The trail ascends up a rocky slope. You'll then make a more gradual ascent to the level, forested top of Lewis Mountain at 0.5 mile; John Lewis, who had a grant of land on the mountain, was a surveyor with George Washington. The trail descends the eastern flank of the Lewis Mountain, but soon gets overgrown and eventually disappears.

Skyline Drive: Beyond Lewis Mountain notice how the trees branch across the Drive forming a canopy. The Oaks Overlook at Mile 59.1 has become overgrown, but you can see the town of Elkton to the left.

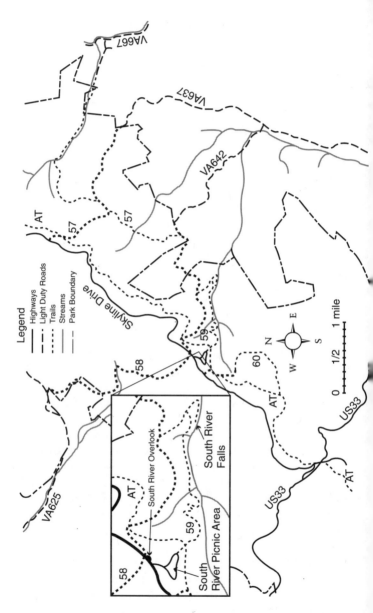

Map 10. Pocosin to Saddleback Mountain

57 Pocosin Trail

2.7 miles one-way
(Pocosin Mission Ruins 1.1 miles one-way)
Moderate
Elevation loss: 800 ft.
Cautions: Can be overgrown, severe flood damage
Connections: AT, Pocosin Hollow Trail,
South River Fire Road

Attractions: You'll pass by the ruins of an Episcopal mission and the South River Cemetery before reaching the South River Fire Road, which can be used for a loop hike.

Trailhead: At mile 59.5, turn east onto the Pocosin Fire Road. You'll see a parking area and the road blocked by a cable.

Description: Walk down the Pocosin Fire Road. At 0.1 mile, the road crosses the AT. To the left, you can walk 1.7 miles to a junction with the Lewis Mountain Trail at the campground. To the right the AT leads 2.9 miles to the South River Fire Road.

Keep straight past the AT. At 0.2 mile, a side road to the right leads up to the Pocosin Cabin, built by the CCC and now maintained by the PATC. The cabin may be rented.

Continue straight on the Pocosin Fire Road, which continues to descend to a junction with the Pocosin Trail on the right at 1.1 miles. The fire road continues straight, where you'll find in 0.2 mile the beginning of the Pocosin Hollow Trail on the left. That trail heads north and east to descend Pocosin Hollow, crossing the stream and emerging from the park in 2.1 miles, crossing the stream again, and connecting with VA667 at 2.8 miles; most of this trail was washed out in the 1995 flood, so take care. The Pocosin Fire Road continues east to reach the park boundary in 1.2 miles and head southeast as VA637.

At the junction with the Pocosin Trail, turn right. Immediately to the left, you'll see the tumble-down ruins of a wooden cabin. Beyond sit the foundations of the old stone Pocosin Mission, with steps leading up to the nonexistent door. These ruins were

Pocosin Ruins

once part of an Episcopal mission, established in 1904 to work within the mountain community that once occupied this area of the park. "Pocosin" is an Indian word meaning a swamp or marsh. Across the trail from the mission site, you'll find the few nameless headstones of an old cemetery.

Continue down the Pocosin Trail, following an old roadbed. The trail can get quite overgrown in late summer. You'll step over several small streams. At 2.1 miles, the trail passes over a rise and drops into a hollow and curves left at a large poplar tree where a stream emerges from rocks below the trail. You'll see here some of the largest trees in the park.

At 2.6 miles, you'll reach a side trail to the left that leads 0.1 mile to the South River Cemetery. This side trail can also be overgrown in summer. Watch for a curve left before you reach the fenced cemetery. You'll find grave markers from the 1800s.

On the main trail, turn right to complete the hike. At 2.7 miles, you'll reach the South River Fire Road at the park boundary. To the left, the South River Fire Road becomes VA642, which at this writing is closed for public access.

You can use the South River Fire Road to the right to complete a 7.7-mile loop hike. Turning right on the South River Road, you'd walk along the park boundary and pass through part of the Rapidan Wildlife Management Area before you reenter the park. This road also can get overgrown in late summer.

Continuing on the road, you'd reach another road to the left at 3.9 miles. You have now joined the South River Falls Loop. To the left, you can reach the end of the South River Falls Trail in 0.4 mile; it's then 0.2 mile up that trail to the overlook for South River Falls (see Trail #59).

To complete this loop hike, you'd continue up the South River Fire Road to a junction with the AT at 4.7 miles. Left on the AT leads 0.5 mile to the beginning of the South River Falls Trail. Straight leads to Skyline Drive in 0.3 mile. Turn right on the AT to complete the loop to the Pocosin Fire Road at 7.6 miles. Left up the road, it's 0.1 mile back to the parking area.

Skyline Drive: From the Baldface Mountain Overlook at Mile 61.3, you'll see Elkton to the left and Dean Mountain, the low ridge in the foreground.

58 Dry Run Falls Fire Road

2.0 miles one-way
Difficult
Elevation loss: 600 ft.
Cautions: Bushwhacking
Connections: None

Attractions: Dry Run Falls is worth the trouble if you're an experienced hiker; all others may enjoy an easy stroll down the road, but do not attempt to search for the falls.

Trailhead: At Mile 62.7 you'll see the Dry Run Falls Fire Road on the right and, just beyond, the South River Overlook where you can park. The view from the overlook is nearly blocked by trees, but you can see to the left the South River Valley and to the right, just over the trees, Saddleback Mountain.

Description: From the South River Overlook parking, walk back up Skyline Drive to Dry Run Falls Fire Road on the west. On the east side of the Drive, the South River Fire Road leads 0.3 mile to the AT and the South River Falls Loop.

Head down the Dry Run Falls Fire Road. At 0.7 mile watch for rock outcrops on the right and a tall cliff. At 1.3 miles the road crosses Dry Run and then bears left to follow the creek downstream. At 1.9 miles, you'll reach a chain across the road blocking vehicle access from outside the park. The road continues, emerging from the park to connect with VA625 in another mile. But the road condition is poor and there's little parking.

Before the chain across the road, turn left to follow an old roadbed. Stay with it, and you'll reach the edge of Dry Run at 2.3 miles. You must then bushwhack your way down Dry Run until you reach the falls at 2.5 miles. You'll pass some spillways in the creek as you descend, but keep going until you reach a cascade of about 20 feet. Because of the off-trail search for the falls, this route should only be attempted by experienced hikers.

🄵🄾 South River Falls Loop

3.3 miles
(South River Falls Overlook 1.3 miles one-way)
Moderate
Elevation change: 1000 ft.
Cautions: Steep downhill
Connections: Appalachian Trail, South River Fire Road

Attractions: You'll descend to an overlook of South River Falls and then to the bottom of this 83-foot waterfall, the third highest in the park. In spring, wildflowers are plentiful.

Trailhead: At mile 62.8, turn east into the South River Picnic Area. You'll soon be on a one-way loop to the right. Watch for the trailhead on your right not long before completing the loop back to the entrance. A sign at the trailhead shows a map of the loop hike. An additional walk to the base of the falls will add another 1.4 miles to the hike, but the view of the falls is well worth the extra distance.

Description: From the trailhead, you'll descend into a hardwood forest. At a little less than 0.1 mile, the trail crosses the AT. You'll complete the loop along the AT from the left. To the right, the AT leads 0.3 mile to an old road that connects with the Saddleback Mountain Trail.

Continue straight on the South River Falls Trail. At 0.4 mile the trail swings left into a switchback right as the trail descends steeply. After three more switchbacks, you'll see on your right at 0.6 mile the upper part of South River. You'll pass a short path that leads right to the stream's edge. At 0.7 mile the trail crosses a side creek flowing under the rocks of the trail.

At 1.0 mile, the trail turns right then left to form an S curve; you'll then be closer to the main stream once again. At 1.1 miles, the trail crosses another side stream; rocks cemented together form a stepping-stone bridge over the trickle of water. Ahead you can see the forest opening up where the land drops away at the waterfall.

Continue to a rock bluff that provides your first view of the falls on your right, and then just beyond at 1.3 miles, you'll reach the overlook for the falls with a rock wall.

From the overlook, the trail ascends with a rock bluff on your left to connect with an old road at 1.5 miles; you'll see a hitching rail on the left. The loop hike continues to the left, but you can walk 0.7 mile to the right to get to the bottom of the falls.

To the right, you'll descend on the road through a curve to the right that skirts the Rapidan Wildlife Management Area outside the park boundary. You'll reach the end of the road in half a mile at the South River. Then take the rocky footpath that leads 0.2 mile upstream to the foot of the waterfall. The path can get overgrown with nettle in late summer. The path ends at the plunge pool; above, the waterfall begins as a single stream that separates halfway down to form two falls of water at the bottom. Return the way you came to ascend back to the main loop.

Back at the junction of the South River Falls Trail with the old road, continue straight, or if you're coming from the overlook and did not go to the bottom of the falls, turn left. At 1.9 miles along the loop route, the old road joins the South River Fire Road. These roads have yellow blazes because they are used as horse trails. To the right the South River Fire Road reaches the Pocosin Trail in 1.2 miles.

Turn left up the South River Fire Road to stay on the loop; some sections are eroded. Ascend along this road until at 2.7 miles the road crosses the AT, blazed white. You can continue straight on the road to reach Skyline Drive in 0.3 mile. Right on the AT, you can walk 2.9 miles north to connect with the Pocosin Fire Road. That route can be used for a 7.7-mile loop hike that incorporates the Pocosin Trail (see Trail #57).

At this junction of the AT and the South River Fire Road, turn left on the AT to complete the loop hike. At 3.2 miles the AT crosses the South River Falls Trail. Turn right to return to the trailhead and picnic area.

South River Falls

⑥⓪ Saddleback Mountain/ AT Loop

3.8 miles
Moderate
Elevation change: 300 ft.
Cautions: Can get overgrown
Connections: Appalachian Trail

Attractions: You'll enjoy an isolated trek through the forest of the Blue Ridge.

Trailhead: Begin at the South River Picnic Area at Mile 62.8 along the South River Falls Trail to the AT.

Description: From the South River Trailhead, descend on the South River Falls Trail to the crossing of the AT at a little less that 0.1 mile. Turn right on the AT. After passing through a woods with several large oaks, you'll reach a junction with a service road at 0.3 mile. To the right in 0.1 mile you would emerge on Skyline Drive at Mile 63.1. Bear left here as the AT follows the service road.

You'll reach a junction where the service road becomes the Saddleback Mountain Trail at 0.5 mile. The AT continues to the right toward Swift Run Gap in 2.4 miles. Bear left, still on the service road.

At 0.8 mile, the road arrives at the PATC South River Maintenance Building; no camping. To the left just before the structure, you'll see a path to a spring.

The trail continues in front of the building, becoming a moss-covered footpath, although still on an old roadbed. From here on the trail is rocky and can get overgrown because it is seldom used; stinging nettle and briers brushed our legs in places.

At 1.1 miles, the trail bears right to begin an ascent. You'll pass an old rail fence on the right from an early settlement. The trail descends to cross a shallow stream at 1.8 miles and then reaches a junction with the AT at 1.9 miles. Turn right to complete the loop.

The AT heads uphill to the north, eventually closing the loop when you reach the junction with the other end of the Saddleback Mountain Trail at 3.3 miles. Turn left up the service road to the junction where the AT turns to the right at 3.5 miles, which you follow back to the South River Falls Picnic Area at 3.8 miles.

Skyline Drive: At Mile 63.1 you'll pass the service road on the east that leads to the AT near the beginning of the Saddleback Mountain Trail. You'll find parking for the Dean Cemetery on the west side of the Drive at Mile 63.2; only authorized persons should enter the cemetery.

From the Hensley Hollow Overlook at Mile 64.4 you'll have a view down Hensley Hollow. You'll pass a pullout on the west at Mile 64.9 and reach Swift Run Gap and access to US33 at Mile 65.5. The highway separates the Central District from the South District.

This highway through Swift Run Gap is also called the "Spottswood Trail" because it was thought to be the gap where Governor Alexander Spottswood crossed the Blue Ridge on his notorious expedition to explore the western part of the Virginia colony. The Spottswood group may have actually crossed the Blue Ridge farther to the north at Milam Gap. You'll see in Swift Run Gap along US33 three monuments to the Spottswood expedition.

The road through Swift Run Gap was an early passage over the Blue Ridge. Improved and made a turnpike in the early 1800s, the road was used by Shenandoah Valley farmers to haul their products east and was also traversed by armies during the Civil War. Lam's Mill stood on the lower east side of the gap along the highway in the early 1900s; it became a gathering place for farmers needing to grind corn and wheat. Once the automobile came along, the Haney store, located in the gap at about where the entrance station is today, added gas pumps, and the Murphy gas station was erected across the highway. On the lower west side of the gap, the brick Mountain Inn, later known as the Shipp Tavern, operated in the 1800s.

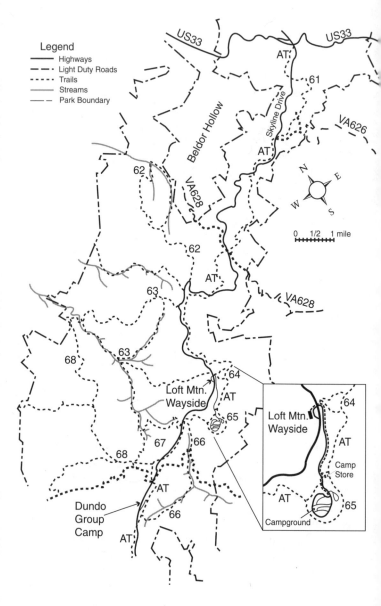

Map 11. Hightop to Jones Run

6̲1̲ Hightop Summit

1.4 miles one-way
Easy
Elevation gain: 950 ft.
Cautions: Rocky sections
Connections: Appalachian Trail

Attractions: The view from the summit of Hightop offers a grand introduction to the South District of the park.

Trailhead: Pull in the parking for Hightop on the west side of Skyline Drive at Mile 66.7. The AT crosses the Drive at the north end of the parking area. It's 1.2 miles back along the AT to Swift Run Gap where the trail crosses US33 on the Drive overpass.

Description: Cross Skyline Drive on the Appalachian Trail to the east side and follow the trail into the woods. You'll bear right and begin the ascent of Hightop Mountain. The trail winds up the mountain with some rocky sections. As we ascended the mountain, we came around a bend to see a bobcat sitting about 50 yards down the trail with its back to us. We stood still; it had not noticed us yet. Eventually it turned and peered at us with curiosity. Then when we made a slight movement, it became frightened and ran, quickly disappearing into the woods.

After a steep section at 0.9 mile, the trail curves right across a level shoulder of the mountain and then curves right again to continue the winding ascent. At 1.3 miles, you'll curve west over another shoulder and then bear left along the edge of the mountain. At rock outcrops, you'll have glimpses to the south; then at 1.4 miles you'll come to a panoramic view of the mountain range to the southwest.

The view provides a good introduction to the park's South District. First find Rocky Mount with exposed rock on its slope straight out from the overlook. Then to the left stands Twomile Ridge, Rockytop, and Rocky Mountain. In the foreground, you'll see the perfectly rounded summit of Roundtop. Then look for the sharp peak of Trayfoot Mountain on the horizon with Blackrock

View from Hightop

to the left, then Loft Mountain, Big Flat Mountain, Little Flat Mountain, Pasture Fence Mountain, Calf Mountain, and Bucks Elbow Mountain.

If you continue south on the AT from the overlook, in 100 yards you'll reach a side trail to the left that leads to the summit of Hightop where a fire lookout tower once stood. At 3587 feet, Hightop is the highest peak in the South District.

On down the AT, you'll pass a spring on the left and descend through masses of purple spiderwort in late spring. At 1.9 miles you'll reach a junction with a trail to the right that leads 0.1 mile to the Hightop Hut and a spring; the hut is reserved for long-distance hikers on the Appalachian Trail. Continuing on the AT, you'll cross the service road to the shelter and recross Skyline Drive at Smith Roach Gap at Mile 68.6 in another 1.3 miles.

Skyline Drive: Continuing south on Skyline Drive from Hightop Parking, you'll reach Swift Run Overlook at Mile 67.2. To the left you'll look west to Beldor Ridge and Hanse Mountain in an arm of the park across Beldor Hollow.

At the Sandy Bottom Overlook at Mile 67.8 you'll look down into Beldor Hollow and the community of Sandy Bottom with Beldor Ridge and Hanse Mountain beyond.

The AT crosses the Drive at Smith Roach Gap at Mile 68.6. There's parking on the east side; you can follow the AT north 1.8 miles to Hightop summit. The Smith Roach Gap Fire Road descends the east side of the mountain to emerge from the park and connect with VA626 in one mile. A spur off this road is the service road for the Hightop Hut.

From the Bacon Hollow Overlook at Mile 69.3 on the east you'll look down Bacon Hollow to a small community. Homes stand below and at the top of Flattop Mountain to the right outside the park. Roundtop Mountain towers over you on the other side of the Drive.

At Powell Gap at Mile 69.9 the AT crosses the Drive once again; there's parking on the east. From the Eaton Hollow Overlook at Mile 70.6 you'll look down into Eaton Hollow, a branch of Beldor Hollow. To the right, you'll see Bush Mountain and farther to the right the obvious rounded top of Roundtop Mountain, the mountain at Bacon Hollow Overlook.

The Rocky Mount Overlook at Mile 71.2 offers a good view of Rocky Mount, the mountain with talus slopes straight out from the overlook. Continuing on the Drive, notice on the east side the numerous white plumes of goat's beard that bloom in June.

From the Beldor Hollow Overlook at Mile 72.2 you'll look into the head of Beldor Hollow to the left. The ridgeline leading right to Rocky Mount is the route of the Rocky Mount Trail.

At Simmons Gap at Mile 73.2 the AT crosses the Drive once again. An old road crosses the gap here; to the west it descends into Beldor Hollow and to the east it descends into Fork Hollow; outside the park on both sides, the old road becomes VA628. Just down the road to the east, you'll find the Simmons Gap Ranger Station.

You'll look down on Shifflett Hollow below the Loft Mountain Overlook at Mile 74.4. Loft Mountain stands to the right.

At Mile 75.2 in Pinefield Gap the AT crosses the Drive. Just beyond the crossing, there's graveled parking next to the service road that leads east to the Pinefield Hut on the AT.

⑥② Rocky Mount/Gap Run Loop

9.8 miles
Moderate
Elevation change: 1500 ft.
Cautions: Steep ascents and descents, creek fords
Connections: None

Attractions: This loop hike explores the peninsula of park land on the west side of Beldor Hollow.

Trailhead: You'll pass the beginning of the Rocky Mount Trail at Mile 76.1 on Skyline Drive; there's no parking at the trailhead. Continue on to the Twomile Run Overlook at Mile 76.2 to park and walk back up the road to pick up the trail. From the overlook, you'll see Twomile Ridge with the hollow of Onemile Run on its left and Twomile Run on its right. Farther right stands Rocky Mount in the distance.

Description: Entering the woods, the Rocky Mount Trail passes over a knoll and heads out along the ridge leading to Rocky Mount. You'll make a winding descent along the ridge until you level off and bear left off the ridgeline at 0.6 mile to circle a knoll. The trail passes through mountain laurel and blueberries. Back to the ridgeline at 0.8 mile, you'll then swing to the right to circle another knoll.

The trail then makes a long but easy descent to a junction with the Gap Run Trail to the right at 2.2 miles. You'll return along that trail from the right; stay straight to begin the ascent of Rocky Mount. At 2.4 miles you'll cross a small talus slope and continue a winding ascent with switchbacks and steep sections; the trail passes by large boulders.

At 3.0 miles, you'll enter a more open area on the ridgeline where the trail turns right to continue the ascent. You'll have a view to the southwest at 3.2 miles, looking across the hollow of Twomile Run to Twomile Ridge. At 3.3 miles you'll reach the summit of Rocky Mount, but there's no view here for the trees.

Now descend the northwest side of Rocky Mount. A step

down a sheet of rock at 3.5 miles signals a steep section. You'll swing back to the ridgeline at 3.7 miles and continue the descent. When we last hiked the trail, small trees and bushes crowded the trail.

At 4.3 miles, the trail turns right in the descent, winding down several switchbacks. You'll encounter a small stream, a tributary of Gap Run; follow it down and crisscross the stream at 4.8 miles. Watch for magnificent stands of cinnamon fern. The trail turns right once again and descends to a ford of Gap Run and leads up to a junction with the Gap Run Trail at 5.3 miles.

To the left, an old road once led to the park boundary in 0.7 mile, but that route is now abandoned. Turn right. The old roadbed becomes rocky before the trail swings off to the right. Upon reaching a clearing, the trail curves left back into the woods. You may hear sounds from Beldor Hollow to your left as the trail skirts the park boundary. At 5.5 miles, you'll pass a trail post where there was once a junction, but no more.

Back on the old roadbed, you'll cross runoff from a slough to the left at 5.9 miles. Soon you'll encounter a rocky flood zone along the creek; head straight into the flood zone and then turn left to pick up the path. On the roadbed again, you'll walk through a wet area where a drainage runs down the trail for a few yards. At 6.1 miles, the trail turns onto another old road.

You'll rockhop Gap Run at 6.4 miles. We surprised a flock of fledgling grouse after this stream crossing; they scattered in all directions while the hen squawked in the undergrowth, trying to draw us away.

As the trail gains elevation, the roadbed narrows and becomes eroded. At 6.6 miles you'll cross Gap Run and continue a winding ascent up the hollow. At 7.0 miles, the trail crosses Gap Run again. You'll continue to ascend, making a steep and rocky climb back to the ridgeline and a junction with the Rocky Mount Trail at 7.6 miles. Now that you've closed the loop, turn left to get back to Skyline Drive in another 2.2 miles.

Skyline Drive: Just beyond the Twomile Run Overlook lies the overgrown trailhead for the Onemile Run Trail, which descends along Onemile Run 3.7 miles to the park boundary; access beyond the boundary is limited.

⑥③ Brown Mountain/Big Run Portal/Rocky Mountain Run Loop

10.1 miles
Moderate
Elevation change: 1625 ft.
Cautions: Steep descents and ascents, rocky, creek fords
Connections: Rockytop Trail

Attractions: This interesting loop takes you over the quartzite cliffs of Rocky Mountain and down to the Big Run Portal.

Trailhead: Park at the Brown Mountain Overlook at Mile 76.9 on Skyline Drive. From the overlook, you'll have a good view of Rocky Mountain with the Erwin quartzite cliffs straight out from the overlook. To the left, you're looking down into the valley of Big Run with Rockytop Ridge beyond. To the right stands Twomile Ridge and Rocky Mount.

Description: To begin the hike, walk through the gap in the center of the wall at the overlook to pick up the Brown Mountain Trail. The path swings left and right from the overlook. You'll continue descending to a left turn at 0.1 mile. The trail then descends out along a ridge with switchbacks to arrive at a junction with the Rocky Mountain Run Trail to the left at 0.7 mile, which will be the return route.

Stay straight past this junction, ascending from the saddle along the right side of a knoll. You'll ascend steeply with switchbacks and reach the peak of the knoll at 1.7 miles. Turn right to continue out the ridgeline. In late May and June, watch for turkeybeard, a clump of white flowers on a tall spike,

Winding up along the ridgeline, you'll reach the crest of Rocky Mountain at 2.3 miles. The trail crosses the top of the white quartzite cliffs you saw from the Brown Mountain Overlook; in fact you can see the overlook to your left along the crest of the Blue Ridge. Across the exposed rock, the trail turns right over the ridgeline to drop off the ridge and begin a winding

173

Turkeybeard

174

descent. The footing is rocky at times.

At 3.2 miles, you'll have a view from the side of Brown Mountain, the lower peak behind Rocky Mountain; the view is to the southwest with the Big Run Valley below and Rockytop ridge beyond. From Brown Mountain, the trail descends to the west and then rises to another knoll at 3.5 miles with rock outcrops. A path up to left in rocks gives a glimpse of the Big Run Valley.

You'll cross a talus slope with views of the Bearwallow Run Valley to the north. The trail continues a winding descent, crosses over the ridgeline among exposed rock, and rises up the last knoll on the ridgeline at 4.1 miles. The trail turns steeply off the right side of the knoll to begin the final descent toward Big Run Portal.

The trail switchbacks down the rocky slope of the ridge, passing a small rocky knoll. You'll swing around the end of the ridge at 4.4 miles and continue a steep, winding descent. At 4.9 miles you'll have a good view of the Big Run Valley and the talus slopes on the side of Rockytop Ridge. Continuing down the rocky trail, you'll have a grand view at 5.1 miles of the passage of Big Run through the mountains, called the "Big Run Portal."

Curving left, you'll wind down to a junction at 5.3 miles. The makeshift path to the right leads to a camping site on Big Run. This is the approximate origin of a fire in 1986 that burned almost 4500 acres in the Big Run watershed; you may notice fire-scarred trees in the area. Turn left a few paces to reach a second junction, here with the Big Run Portal Trail.

To the right, the Big Run Portal Trail crosses a metal bridge over Big Run, a large creek because it drains the largest watershed in the park. The trail then heads down Big Run along an old roadbed where you can glimpse the rock walls of the portal of Big Run through the trees. The trail connects with the bottom end of the Rockytop Trail in 0.5 mile and reaches the park boundary in 0.7 mile. There's no public access from outside the park.

To continue this loop hike, head left on the Big Run Portal Trail, which follows the rocky roadbed east up the mountain. At 5.6 miles you'll ford Big Run to the south side. The trail fords the creek again at 6.0 miles and soon after crosses a side stream. The trail can get a bit overgrown in summer along the creek.

You'll ford again at 6.4 miles and 6.6 miles. You'll then reach a junction with the Rocky Mountain Run Trail to the left at 6.7 miles. The Big Run Portal Trail continues up Big Run, fording Rocky Mountain Run to connect with the Patterson Ridge Trail in 0.2 mile and fording Big Run three more times to connect with the Big Run Loop in 2.3 miles.

Turn left on the Rocky Mountain Run Trail to complete the loop hike. The trail follows an old roadbed to parallel Rocky Mountain Run. At 7.2 miles a rock shelf in the creekbed creates a three-foot fall of water into a good wading pool for a hot summer day. You'll ford Rocky Mountain Run at 7.4 miles. By the time you cross again at 8.1 miles the stream is small enough to rockhop. Soon after, you'll cross back over the stream as you continue up the hollow.

As you ascend, the stream has less and less water until the streambed is dry, unless there have been recent rains. The trail becomes rocky as the hollow narrows, and you follow the streambed up. At 9.0 miles, the trail becomes steep in a series of switchbacks that take you up the ridge to a junction with the Brown Mountain Trail to close the loop at 9.4 miles. Turn right to get back to the Brown Mountain Overlook in another 0.7 mile.

Skyline Drive: The AT passes through the Ivy Creek Overlook at Mile 77.5. The view east includes Flattop Mountain and Hightop to the left and Loft Mountain to the right.

At the Rockytop Overlook at Mile 78.1 you'll have a view of the Big Run watershed. To the west you'll see Rockytop with talus slopes and, to the right, Brown Mountain and Rocky Mountain. Far to the left stands the peak of Trayfoot Mountain.

The service road to the Ivy Creek Maintenance Hut drops off Skyline Drive to the east at Mile 79.4. On the west side of the Drive you'll see the marker for the Patterson Ridge Trail, which heads out along Patterson Ridge to descend to the Big Run Portal Trail in 3.1 miles. There is no parking here; so if you want to hike the Patterson Ridge Trail, continue on to the Loft Mountain Wayside on the west side of Skyline Drive at Mile 79.5 where there is ample parking.

Big Run

⑥④ Deadening Nature Trail Loop

1.1 miles
Moderate
Elevation change: 500 ft.
Cautions: Steep ascent and descent
Connections: Appalachian Trail

Attractions: You'll find one of the finest views in the park and a profusion of blooming phacelia in late May and June.

Trailhead: Park at the Loft Mountain Wayside at Mile 79.5. You'll find there a snack bar, giftshop, gas, restrooms and telephone; it's closed in the off-season. Across the Drive from the wayside, a road leads up the mountain to the Loft Mountain Campground/Picnic Area, which is actually on Big Flat Mountain; Loft Mountain stands just to the north. To hike the Deadening Nature Trail, walk to the north from the wayside on the sidewalk to cross the Drive to the east side.

Description: A few yards up from Skyline Drive, the Deadening Nature Trail begins on the left; the paved path continues up the mountain, following the road to the campground. As soon as you turn left on the nature trail, you'll encounter a fork; to hike the loop clockwise, take the left fork.

The trail ascends steeply with switchbacks up to a rock wall at 0.3 mile where you'll bear right along the wall. The trail then turns left to get above the wall and continue the ascent. At 0.4 mile, you'll cross an expanse of bare rock. Turn right out to the rock edge for one of the best views in the park. You're looking west, with Skyline Drive below and Rockytop Ridge in the distance to the left. Below to the right you'll see the Big Run Valley and the portal and farther to the right Brown Mountain and Rocky Mountain and far to the right the peak of Loft Mountain.

The nature trail bears left from the overlook to a junction with the Appalachian Trail. To the left the AT passes through a more open area that was once grazing land to a rock outcrop in 0.3 mile with a view east and then past the peak of Loft Mountain

Deadening Nature Trail view

in 0.7 mile before beginning a descent toward Ivy Creek Spring.

To continue on the Deadening Nature Trail Loop, turn right on the AT. In June, masses of pale blue phacelia line the trail, making it a beautiful walk. You'll soon pass a path up to a rock outcrop and another view west, virtually the same view as the previous overlook on the nature trail. You'll reach a junction at 0.5 mile with the nature trail turning right; the AT continues straight to descend through a gap and then ascend to the Loft Mountain Campground on Big Flat Mountain in 1.3 miles.

Turn right on the nature trail. You'll make a steep descent through a more open area that was once Patterson Fields where cattle grazed in the early 1900s; the Patterson family drove their cattle from the Shenandoah Valley up the route of the Patterson Ridge Trail. Land was cleared for grazing by girdling the trees, which of course caused them to die and allowed light to penetrate to the forest floor. Later, when they had time and needed wood or lumber, the farmers would come back for the standing dead trees, which was called a "deadening." If the trees were never harvested, they would eventually fall and decompose on the ground.

The trail reenters more mature forest and continues a descent to close the loop at 1.1 miles. Turn right on the paved path to cross back over Skyline Drive to the Loft Mountain Wayside.

⑥⑤ Loft Mountain Campground Loop

1.6 miles
Easy
Elevation change: 100 ft.
Cautions: None
Connections: Appalachian Trail

Attractions: If you're staying at Loft Mountain Campground, this hike offers a pleasant walk with sunset views after you've set up camp.

Trailhead: There are several access points from the campground area on Big Flat Mountain to this loop trail. We start the description from the amphitheater parking. Turn up the road that leads to the campground across from the Loft Mountain Wayside at Mile 79.5. After you pass the turnoff left to the campground store, which has food and showers for campers, turn in the parking area on the right.

Description: You'll see the paved path leading down from the campground toward the wayside on Skyline Drive. There's also a paved walk that leads ahead to the amphitheater. Walk down that path a few paces to turn left on a grassy trail that's the beginning of the loop. At 0.1 mile you'll reach a junction with the AT, which heads south to Browns Gap in 3.0 miles. Turn left on the AT to circle the backside of the campground.

The AT makes some short, steep ascents to get on a level with the campground and reach a junction at 0.3 mile. From the left, you can walk down from near tentsite A-8 for 0.1 mile to cross the AT here and walk down to an overlook to the right that offers a good location to watch the sunset, with Blackrock and Trayfoot Mountains to the south.

At 0.5 mile, you'll skirt the back of the campground near site A-14 where it's a short walk down to cross the AT for views to the southwest, another good spot for watching the day end.

Continue around the campground through a forest thick with fern to a side trail to the left at 0.8 mile that's another access from the campground to the AT. At 0.9 mile you'll pass some paths on the left that lead up to the picnic area.

The trail then heads downhill to reach a junction with a trail to the left that leads up to the camp store at 1.4 miles. The AT continues straight to eventually link up with the Deadening Nature Trail in 1.0 mile. Turn left up to the camp store to complete this loop hike. You'll ascend steeply to the store where an expanse of grass offers a view to the east.

Pick up the paved walk that passes beside the store. Out front, you'll connect at 1.5 miles with the paved path that leads down from the campground to the wayside. Turn left up the paved path to pass in front of the store, cross Skyline Drive, and return to the amphitheater parking at 1.6 miles.

66 Doyles River/Jones Run/ AT Loop

7.8 miles
Moderate
Elevation change: 1400 ft.
Cautions: Stream fords, steep sections, highway crossings
Connections: Appalachian Trail, Browns Gap Fire Road,
Madison Run Fire Road, Big Run Loop

Attractions: This is one of our favorite hikes, with the upper and lower Doyles River Falls and Jones Run Falls.

Trailhead: Pull in the Doyles River Parking Area at Mile 81.1 on the east side of Skyline Drive.

Description: At the far right of the parking area, you'll see the trailhead where the Doyles River Trail begins. The trail descends, crossing the Appalachian Trail, which to the right will be the return route for this loop hike. To the left the AT leads 1.2 miles north to the Loft Mountain Campground.

Continuing downhill on the Doyles River Trail you'll pass a spring on the left at 0.3 mile and soon after reach a fork with a side trail left up to the Doyles River Cabin, which may be rented from the PATC. To continue on the Doyles River Trail, take the right fork.

At 0.5 mile, you'll cross a creek on stepping stones. You'll step over a small creek at 0.8 mile that's probably dry in summer. Soon you'll parallel Doyles River on the right. The trail crosses Browns Gap Fire Road at 0.9 mile. To the right the road crosses Doyles River on a metal bridge and ascends to Skyline Drive in 1.8 miles at Browns Gap at Mile 83.0. To the left the road descends the mountain to emerge from the park in 1.5 miles and become VA629.

Stay straight on the Doyles River Trail. You'll soon cross Doyles River on stones and continue down along the river to pass a small drop and then reach the head of the upper falls of the Doyles River at 1.2 miles. On down the trail, you'll swing right and left, rockhop a small stream, and reach a junction with a side trail left that leads down to the bottom of this upper falls, a two-step cascade of water 28 feet high. Notice the large tulip poplars nearby.

Continue down the trail from the turnoff for the upper falls. Just before reaching the lower falls, you'll pass a rock wall on the right that in late May is covered in pale blue phacelia. After, you'll switchback left and descend to the lower falls of the Doyles River at 1.5 miles, a 63-foot cascade of water.

The trail switchbacks right at a view of the falls and continues to descend along Doyles River, which contains more cascades and spillways. At 1.7 miles, you'll cross a bridge over a steeply cascading stream that's a tributary of the river. Watch for a huge tulip poplar beside the trail at 2.0 miles. The large trees, cascading streams, waterfalls, and oodles of wildflowers make this a perfect hike on a sunny spring day.

You'll reach a junction with the Jones Run Trail at 2.1 miles. Turn right up along Jones Run. At 2.2 miles the trail fords Jones Run and continues upstream. Notice the large poplars and oaks along this stretch.

The trail ascends more steeply and becomes rocky at 2.6 miles. You'll cross a side stream on rocks. Notice a nice water slide in Jones Run on the way up. At 2.8 miles the trail reaches Jones Run Falls, a 42-foot drop that's part cascade, part waterfall.

You'll switchback left at the bottom of the falls to continue ascending the trail. Up past massive blocks of stone, you'll switchback right to get above the falls where an unofficial path to the right leads to the top of the falls; take care.

The trail continues to ascend along Jones Run through patches of wild geranium in late spring and past big trees and big rocks. At 3.2 miles, watch for where Jones Run breaks into a multitude of rivulets among rocks in the streambed; soon after, a path right leads to a pool in the stream where you can get your feet wet.

You'll ascend more steeply and then level off to swing right and rockhop the upper part of Jones Run at 4.0 miles. Ascending again, the trail switchbacks left at 4.2 miles and crosses the trace of a road that's the right-of-way for the waterline to the nearby

Doyles River Falls

Jones Run Falls

186

Dundo Group Camp. At 4.5 miles you'll reach a junction with the Appalachian Trail at the Jones Run Parking Area at Mile 84.1 on Skyline Drive. To the left the AT leads south 1.3 miles to Blackrock. Turn right on the AT to complete this loop hike.

At 5.1 miles the AT skirts the backside of the Dundo Group Camp; a path to the left leads up to the camp. Stay straight on the AT to descend into Browns Gap at Mile 83.0 on Skyline Drive at 5.7 miles. Cross the Drive to the right and enter the parking area for the Madison Run Fire Road on the west side of the Drive. Notice on the east side of the Drive the Browns Gap Fire Road has ascended to here from the Doyles River Trail.

Follow the AT where it turns up right from the Madison Run Fire Road parking area. The trail ascends a dry south-facing slope with laurel, oaks, and blueberry bushes. At 6.3 miles, you'll reach a junction with the Big Run Loop to the left; stay straight on the AT.

You'll descend to cross Skyline Drive to the left at 6.6 miles. Now on the east side of the Drive, the trail drops to the right of a rock outcrop. At 6.8 miles, the AT emerges at the Doyles River Overlook at Mile 81.9 on the Drive. Walk straight through the overlook and pick up the trail again at the far back corner of the parking area.

Back into the woods, the AT continues to parallel the Drive until it reaches a junction with the Doyles River Trail at 7.8 miles below the Doyles River Parking Area. Turn left up the trail to get back to your starting point.

67 Big Run Loop

5.8 miles
Easy
Elevation change: 1100 ft.
Cautions: Stream crossings
Connections: Big Run Portal Trail, Rockytop Trail,
Madison Run Spur Trail, Appalachian Trail,
Doyles River Trail

Attractions: In spring, blooming bushes line this trail into the Big Run watershed.

Trailhead: The Big Run Loop begins at the Big Run Overlook at Mile 81.2. There's better parking at the Doyles River Parking Area at Mile 81.1, and since the loop passes through that parking area, we begin our description there.

Description: From the parking area, walk south on Skyline Drive and cross to the Big Run Overlook on the west side at 0.1 mile; take care along the highway. At the overlook, walk through the gap in the rock wall and pick up the Big Run Loop that descends to the left.

At 0.3 mile, the trail switchbacks right in the descent. You'll pass through pinxter-flower and deerberry blooming in spring and laurel blooming in early summer. In a saddle at 0.7 mile between the main Blue Ridge and a small knoll to the west, the trail curves back left in the descent. You'll soon begin to round the head of a hollow and cross a tributary of Big Run at 1.2 miles. Watch for plenty of crested dwarf iris through this section.

The trail then heads out along a ridge between the tributary and Big Run. At 1.8 miles the trail curves left off the ridge to descend to a rockhop of Big Run at 2.2 miles; notice to the left two streams converge to create Big Run. Switchback right up from the creek to a junction at 2.3 miles with the Big Run Portal Trail to the right. Down that trail, it's 2.1 miles to the Patterson Ridge Trail, 2.3 miles to the Rocky Mountain Run Trail, 3.7 miles to the Brown Mountain Trail, and 4.2 miles to a junction with the Rockytop Trail. Several loop hikes can be made using these trails.

Turn left at this junction to stay on the Big Run Loop. You'll notice along the trail standing dead trees, killed by gypsy moth caterpillars.

Ascending, you'll switchback left at 2.4 miles and right at 3.2 miles. The trail continues by curving left to a four-way junction at 3.6 miles. The Rockytop Trail leads to the right to connect with the Big Run Portal Trail in 5.7 miles. Ahead, the Madison Run Spur Trail leads 0.3 mile to Madison Run Fire Road. Turn left up along the ridge to continue on the Big Run Loop. You'll reach a junction with the Appalachian Trail at 4.3 miles. Turn left on the AT to complete the loop.

You'll descend to cross Skyline Drive to the left at 4.6 miles. Now on the east side of the Drive, the trail drops to the right of a rock outcrop. At 4.8 miles, the AT emerges at the Doyles River Overlook at Mile 81.9 on the Drive. Walk straight through the overlook and pick up the trail again at the far back corner of the parking area.

Back into the woods, the AT continues to parallel the Drive until it reaches a junction with the Doyles River Trail at 5.8 miles below the Doyles River Parking Area. Turn left up the trail to get back to your starting point.

Skyline Drive: At Mile 81.2, the Big Run Overlook offers a panoramic view of the Big Run Valley that drains eleven square miles, the largest watershed in the park. The low notch in the distant mountains is the Big Run Portal, with Rockytop to the left and Brown and Rocky Mountains to the right. The Big Run Loop Trail descends to the left on the outside of the overlook rock wall.

On the east side of the Drive, you'll find the Doyles River Overlook at Mile 81.9. The AT passes through the overlook parking area. The hollow below the overlook is the Doyles River Valley; Jones Run Hollow runs to the right. On the left is Browns Cove, and the prominent peak outside the park is High Top Mountain (not the Hightop on the AT to the north).

The AT crosses the Drive at Mile 82.2. There's no parking.

⑥⑧ Rockytop Trail

6.8 miles one-way
(Views from Rockytop 4.6 miles one-way)
Moderate
Elevation loss: 1500 ft.
Cautions: Talus slope crossings, long descent
Connections: Big Run Loop, Austin Mountain Trail,
Lewis Peak Trail, Big Run Portal Trail.

Attractions: Out along Rockytop Ridge, you'll have fine views to the southwest.

Trailhead: In Browns Gap at Mile 83.0, the AT crosses the Drive. The Browns Gap Fire Road, heading east down the ridge to connect with the Doyles River Trail, and the Madison Run Fire Road on the west were once a turnpike built through the gap in 1806 following an old trail that had long been used. The gap was named for the Brown family that once owned much land on the east side of the mountains. Stonewall Jackson's troops camped in Browns Gap for a week during his Civil War Valley Campaign.

The AT heads north from the parking area at Madison Run Fire Road to connect with the Big Run Loop where you would turn left to reach the beginning of the Rockytop Trail in a total of 1.3 miles. But for a little shorter access, head down the Madison Run Fire Road, which is blocked to vehicles by a chain.

Directions: In 0.8 mile, where the Madison Run Fire Road curves right, turn right off the road onto the Madison Run Spur Trail; the fire road continues down the mountain to emerge from the park as VA663 in 4.3 miles. The Spur Trail to the right ascends to a four-way junction with the Big Run Loop at 1.1 miles. The Rockytop Trail heads left, ascending over a knoll and then another. The trail descends to a junction at 1.5 miles with the Austin Mountain Trail left, which runs southwest over Austin Mountain and descends to a junction with the Madison Run Fire Road in 3.2 miles. Bear right to continue on the Rockytop Trail.

Out along Rockytop Ridge, the trail eventually reaches a
190

junction at 3.3 miles with the Lewis Peak Trail, which heads west past Lewis Peak and descends to the park boundary in 2.6 miles; there's no access from outside the park. At Lewis Peak, a side trail leads to the summit for a view west.

From the junction with the Lewis Peak Trail, the Rockytop Trail bears right down a rocky slope and soon turns right in a long descent and then begins an ascent of the peak of Rockytop. You'll cross a talus slope at 3.7 miles in the ascent that offers a view of Big Run Valley on the right and the Lewis Run Hollow on the left. To the far left stands Lewis Peak, and straight ahead on the left is the next peak along Rockytop Ridge.

The trail makes a long descent from Rockytop, with the next peak looming before you at 2856 feet. In fact, this next peak is a couple of hundred feet higher than the one called "Rockytop" you've just covered. From the saddle between the two peaks, you'll ascend the left side of the second peak. The trail crosses talus slopes. At 4.6 miles, you'll cross a wide talus slope offering a view across Lewis Run Hollow to Lewis Peak and to the left Lewis Mountain and Austin Mountain—of course, a different Lewis Mountain than the one in the Central District.

After circling the peak, you'll begin an ascent with switchbacks to the reach the ridgeline at 4.8 miles. The trail then descends, eventually dropping off the ridge in switchbacks to reach a junction with the Big Run Portal Trail at 6.8 miles.

Skyline Drive: At Mile 83.7 the Dundo Overlook offers a view to the west; look for blooming mountain laurel in June. Dundo Hollow containing Madison Run lies below the overlook with Furnace Mountain to the left and the peak of Austin Mountain to the right. Farther right stands Lewis Mountain and Rockytop Ridge. To the far left stands the peak of Trayfoot Mountain.

You'll pass the turnoff on the east for the Dundo Group Camp at Mile 83.7; contact the park headquarters for reservations. This was once the site of CCC Camp No. 27.

At Mile 84.1, the Jones Run Parking Area lies on the east side of the Drive. Here you can access the Doyles River-Jones Run Loop for short access to Jones Run Falls in 1.7 miles. The AT crosses the Drive at Mile 84.3.

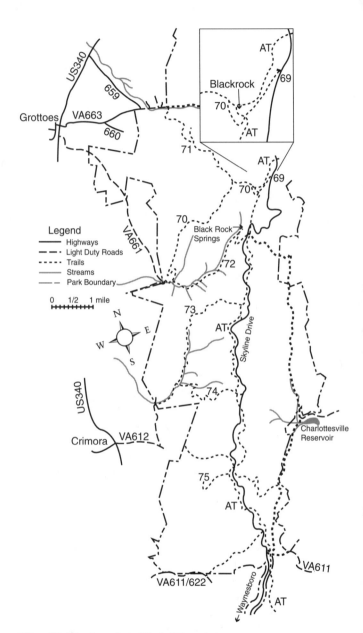

Map 12. Blackrock to Turk Mountain

192

⑥⑨ Blackrock Summit Loop

1.0 mile
Easy
Elevation change: 200 ft.
Cautions: Talus slopes
Connections: Trayfoot Mountain Trail, AT,
Blackrock Spur Trail

Attractions: Outstanding views circle the summit of Blackrock.

Trailhead: On the west side of the Drive, you'll find the Blackrock Summit Parking Area at Mile 84.8.

Directions: The Trayfoot Mountain Trail begins on the left of the parking area, where it follows an old road uphill. You'll ascend steeply to a junction at 0.1 mile where the trail touches the Appalachian Trail on the right; the AT passed just below the parking area to reach this juncture. The Trayfoot Mountain Trail bypasses Blackrock Summit, and so you must get over onto the AT and continue ascending.

At 0.5 mile, the trail emerges at Blackrock, a huge jumble of boulders forming a mountain peak; a talus slope to the right offers a view northwest to Madison Run in Dundo Hollow. Take care if you climb the peak to the left for a wider view. The rock's gray appearance is due to rock tripe, a lichen that grows on the rock. There's also a Blackrock in the Central District.

The AT circles the summit of Blackrock to a junction with the Blackrock Spur Trail that leads 0.1 mile down to a junction with the Trayfoot Mountain Trail. Continue circling the summit for views to the southwest down Paine Run Hollow.

You'll reenter the woods and reach a junction at 0.6 mile where the AT crosses the old road that is the Trayfoot Mountain Trail, which circles below the Blackrock Summit to the right. The AT continues straight toward the Blackrock Hut in half a mile and Blackrock Gap in 1.1 miles. Turn left on the Trayfoot Mountain Trail to return to the Blackrock Parking Area at 1.0 mile.

View from Blackrock summit

70 Trayfoot Mountain Trail

5.4 miles one-way
Moderate
Elevation loss: 1950 ft.
Cautions: Overgrown in places
Connections: Appalachian Trail, Blackrock Spur Trail,
Furnace Mountain Trail, Paine Run Trail

Attractions: You'll cross the summit of Trayfoot Mountain and have a good view of the mountain of Buzzard Rock.

Trailhead: Begin at the Blackrock Summit Parking Area at Mile 84.8.

Description: The Trayfoot Mountain Trail begins at the left side of the parking area where it follows an old road uphill. At 0.1 mile, you'll reach a junction where the AT skirts the road on the right; you can get over on the AT here to get to the summit of Blackrock in 0.4 mile.

Continue straight on the Trayfoot Mountain Trail. At 0.4 mile, you'll reach a junction with the AT. To the left the AT leads toward the Blackrock Hut in 0.5 mile and Blackrock Gap in 1.1 miles. To the right the AT leads around Blackrock Summit. Stay straight on the old road, which now descends as it begins to circle below Blackrock. In a hundred yards you'll pass another old road on the left that leads back toward the AT. Stay straight on the Trayfoot Mountain Trail, and you'll cross a talus slope below Blackrock and ascend to a junction at 0.6 mile with the Blackrock Spur Trail on the right. This spur trail leads 0.1 mile up to the AT on the Blackrock Summit.

Stay straight on the old road as it descends. You'll see plenty of wildflowers in spring along the roadway, but it can tend to get overgrown in summer. The trail drops through a sag in the ridge and continues uphill. When we last passed this way, a sound attracted our attention, and we turned to see to two bear cubs scrambling up a tree. We quickly scrambled away ourselves; the mother was surely nearby watching us and ready to protect her cubs.

You'll reach a junction with the Furnace Mountain Trail to the right at 1.4 miles. That trail leads out along the ridge to the Furnace Mountain Summit and then descends to Madison Run in 3.4 miles. The Trayfoot Mountain Trail curves left at the junction with the Furnace Mountain Trail and continues ascending. You'll reach the summit of Trayfoot Mountain at 1.6 miles. The odd name of the mountain came from the footprints of a bear; a hunter tracking the animal across the mountain said they were nearly as big as a "dough-tray."

The trail now heads out along the ridgeline where you'll have occasional views of Paine Run Hollow below. As you follow the ridgeline, you'll first head west and then south in a big curve you'll hardly notice. The trail has some up and down along the ridge with a thick covering of grass. In some steeper sections, the trail switchbacks in the descents. You'll pass rocky knolls and lichen-covered blocks of stone along the ridgeline.

At 4.6 miles you'll reach a point of the ridge that offers a view west out to farmland of the Shenandoah Valley and left across Paine Run to Buzzard Rock, a perfect cone-shaped mountain from this perspective. The trail swings left past rock outcrops to descend off the ridge. You'll look across Lefthand Hollow to Horsehead Mountain, and then the trail switchbacks right in the descent, dropping to a junction with the Paine Run Trail at 5.4 miles.

To the right the Paine Run Trail leads 0.3 mile to the park boundary. To the left, the trail heads up Paine Run to reach Skyline Drive at Blackrock Gap in 3.4 miles. You can pick up the AT there to make a circuit hike back to the Trayfoot Mountain Trail for a total loop of 9.9 miles and back to Blackrock Parking at 10.3 miles.

7️⃣1️⃣ **Furnace Mountain Trail**

3.4 miles one-way
(Furnace Mountain Summit 2.2 miles one-way)
Moderate
Elevation gain: 2000 ft.
Cautions: Creek ford, long ascent
Connections: Madison Run Fire Road,
Trayfoot Mountain Trail

Attractions: Hiking the trail from the western park boundary, you'll see the Mt. Vernon Furnace at the trailhead and have a great view from the summit of Furnace Mountain.

Trailhead: From Skyline Drive, you'd walk 1.4 miles along the Trayfoot Mountain Trail from the Blackrock Summit Parking Area at Mile 84.8 to get to the beginning of the Furnace Mountain Trail. The Mt. Vernon Furnace, for which the mountain is named, lies on the western boundary; so we recommend hiking from that end. In Grottoes on US340, turn east on VA663. You'll pass VA660 on the right at 1.2 miles and VA659 on the left at 2.2 miles. The road crosses Madison Run and then passes a gravel road to the left at 2.5 miles. Watch for two houses on the left at 2.6 miles; the Mt. Vernon Furnace stands in the woods across the creek on your right just past the second house. With leaves on the trees, you'll have trouble seeing the furnace, a pyramid of large blocks of stone, used for smelting iron. You'll pass a gravel road to the left at 2.7 miles, and then at 2.8 miles you'll find a dirt road to the left at a wide place in the road where you can pull over on the right and park. Do not drive any farther up the road, because there's no place to turnaround.

You can walk back up the road to the furnace where you can glimpse it through the trees. Cross the creek to get to it only at low water. The furnace was built around 1830 and operated until the Civil War and only sporadically afterward. The entire operation included an office building, the superintendent's house, and cabins for the workers. The iron ore was hauled from six mines in the area. The furnace chamber was filled with ore, limestone

197

that removed impurities, and charcoal for the fire. Carbon monoxide from the burning charcoal combined with oxygen in the ore to leave pure iron. The molten iron flowed out into holes dug in the surrounding sand and solidified into pigs of iron, which were then hauled to a foundry at Port Republic.

Description: From the parking space, walk up the road, which becomes the Madison Run Fire Road inside the park. At 0.1 mile, you pass around a chain gate to enter the park. Soon after, you'll reach a junction with the Furnace Mountain Trail on the right. The Madison Run Fire Road continues straight to ascend the ridge and emerge on Skyline Drive in 5.0 miles at Browns Gap.

Turn right on the Furnace Mountain Trail, and you'll ford Madison Run at 0.2 mile. The trail then turns right and soon begins an ascent of Furnace Mountain in a broad curve to the left. Along the south-facing slope of the mountain, you'll see a profusion of mountain laurel and frequent blueberry.

At 1.0 mile, the trail curves right through the head of a hollow and continues ascending. You'll swing around the side of the mountain to the left at 1.4 miles where you'll see ahead a saddle between two peaks of Furnace Mountain. The trail crosses a talus slope and ascends to the saddle and a junction at 1.7 miles. To the left, a side trail leads up through rocks and across talus slopes over the summit of Furnace Mountain in 0.5 mile and steeply down to a rock outcrop that offers a view to the north. You'll see Austin Mountain to the left and its long ridge running up to the Blue Ridge. Rockytop stands at a distance in the center of the view, and between Rockytop and Austin, Lewis Mountain just peaks over the shoulder of Austin Mountain.

From the saddle at the junction, the Furnace Mountain Trail ascends the right-hand peak and continues up the ridge, passing over two more knolls along the way, eventually connecting with the Trayfoot Mountain Trail at 3.4 miles on Trayfoot Mountain.

Skyline Drive: From the Trayfoot Mountain Overlook at Mile 86.8, you'll look east down a hollow to the North Fork of the Moormans River. Far to the right, you can see west over Blackrock Gap to the Shenandoah Valley.

The AT crosses the Drive at Mile 87.2.

198

View from Furnace Mountain

72 Paine Run Trail

3.7 miles one-way
(Black Rock Springs 1.1 miles one-way)
Easy (Difficult exploring hotel site)
Elevation loss: 900 ft.
Cautions: Creekbed crossings
Connections: Appalachian Trail,
North Fork of Moormans River Fire Road,
Trayfoot Mountain Trail

Attractions: The site of the Black Rock Springs Hotel can still be found on a side path as you descend the mountain.

Trailhead: You'll find parking on the west side of the Drive in Blackrock Gap at Mile 87.4. The AT passes by on the east side of the Drive, so if you're walking a loop with the Trayfoot Mountain Trail and the Paine Run Trail, you'd cross the Drive here to get on the AT and head north back to the Trayfoot Mountain Trail in 1.3 miles. Also on the east, you'll see a fire road that descends to the North Fork of the Moormans River outside the park; that road then heads south through the park toward the Charlottesville Reservoir; the lower reaches of the road were washed away in the 1995 flood. The old road that passed through Blackrock Gap is now the Paine Run Trail on the west side of the Drive.

Description: From the parking area, follow the old road down the west side of the mountain. At 0.6 mile, the road curves right in the descent. Then at 1.0 mile, the road curves back left. In this second curve, you'll see the trace of a road heading off to the right. This old road once led to the Black Rock Springs Hotel. You can explore this area, although the going can get a little rough because the way is no longer maintained. The path following the roadbed gets overgrown, and trees have fallen across the trail. About 0.1 mile in, you'll find some foundations and a walled-in spring.

There was a hotel of some sort at this site as early as 1835,

Black Rock Springs

53 years before George F. Pollock held his first camp on Stony Man Mountain. The place served as a summer retreat for visitors from coastal Virginia and Baltimore and Philadelphia. The resort had various owners and changed much over the years. It was taken over by the Black Rock Springs Improvement Company in the 1880s and reached its peak with two rows of cottages curving around a three-story hotel. There were seven springs touted as curing various ailments. A fire in 1909 swept through the forest, taking the hotel and cottages with it. A nearby boarding house was not destroyed and it later became known as the Black Rock Spring Hotel, which survived until the park was established.

Continuing down the old road that's the Paine Run Trail, you'll see across Paine Run Hollow to Horsehead Mountain on your right. As you parallel Paine Run, you'll cross small drainages that flow toward the creek. At 2.8 miles, you'll cross Paine Run to the right. Sometimes the creekbed is dry at this location, with the water flowing under the rocks; sometimes you'll have to ford. Continue down the run, which at the lower elevations has nice pools and spillways.

You'll cross the stream that flows out of Lefthand Hollow and reach a junction with the Trayfoot Mountain Trail at 3.4 miles. The Paine Run Trail, the Trayfoot Mountain Trail, and the Appalachian Trail make a good 9.9-mile loop hike.

The Paine Run Trail continues down the old road, crossing the run two more times and reaching the park boundary at 3.7 miles. The trail emerges from the park at a junction of VA661 and VA614; there's access from outside the park on VA661 only.

Skyline Drive: At the Horsehead Overlook at Mile 88.6, you'll look across Paine Run Hollow, with Horsehead Mountain beyond and Buzzard Rock in the distance. The closer peak to the left is Calvary Rocks, and Trayfoot Mountain stands to the right. On the east side of the Drive, you'll see good exposure of phyllite and sandstone of the Hampton formation.

The AT crosses the Drive at Mile 88.9.

7₃ Riprap Trail

3.6 miles one-way
(Calvary Rocks 1.4 miles one-way)
Moderate
Elevation loss: 1300 ft.
Cautions: Rock bluffs, stream fords
Connections: Appalachian Trail, Wildcat Ridge Trail

Attractions: You'll have views from Calvary Rocks and Chimney Rock, and at the lower end in June, you'll see blooming Catawba rhododendron that peak around Memorial Day weekend.

Trailhead: Pull in the Riprap Parking Area at Mile 90.0 on the west side of Skyline Drive.

Description: At the end of the parking area, take the short path that ascends to the AT. Turn right and ascend through azalea and mountain laurel to a junction with the Riprap Trail on the left at 0.4 mile. The AT continues north to Blackrock Gap in 2.2 miles.

Turn left down the Riprap Trail. You'll curve right into a long descent into a sag and then ascend over a knoll at 0.9 mile. Down again, curving left and right, you'll drop through a saddle and then ascend over another knoll at 1.2 miles. The trail then descends into another sag among exposed rock that looks similar to riprap, rock that's thrown down to shore up and prevent erosion.

You'll ascend for a third time, toward the left and up to the ridge at Calvary Rocks at 1.4 miles. A path to the right takes you out to the rock bluff with a view to the northwest across Paine Run to Horsehead Mountain. The trail continues out along the rocky ridge, through a field of boulders standing on end at 1.5 miles, and finally to a path on the right at 1.6 miles that leads out to a view northwest at Chimney Rock. The iron pegs in the rocks once held a small bridge to the top of Chimney Rock.

The trail curves left at Chimney Rock and descends through laurel to once more reach the edge of the mountain at 2.0 miles for another view across Paine Run Hollow with Buzzard Rock to the left. Soon after, the trail begins a descent off the ridge into Cold Spring Hollow. At 2.4 miles, the trail swings right in the descent. As you continue down, watch for a rock beside the trail with a tree growing on top that makes a good spot for lunch. Notice the huge oak on the left past the rock bench.

At first, the streambed in Cold Spring Hollow is dry, with the water running under the rocks in dry seasons. But as you descend farther, the water emerges and tall cinnamon ferns stand along the creek. At 3.0 miles, you'll enter a small canyon where the stream you've been following joins the main stream running from the left down Riprap Hollow. Just after the confluence, a small waterfall drops a few feet in the streambed.

At 3.1 miles, the Riprap Trail turns up to the right were an abandoned section of trail stays along the creek. The trail then swings back down to the creek and picks up the original trail. As you continue to descend Riprap Hollow, notice the Catawba rhododendron that bloom rose-purple in late May and June; this rhododendron is frequent in the Blue Ridge to the south but only grows on lower elevations this far north.

You'll ford the stream at 3.3 miles to continue down the left side and soon after pass a cascade splashing into a green pool. The trail then fords back across the stream.

Continue straight down the rocky shore that was once an old roadway along the stream. You'll reach a junction at 4.0 miles with the Wildcat Ridge Trail to the left. The Riprap and Wildcat Ridge Trails along with the AT make a good loop hike of 9.3 miles.

The Riprap Trail continues down along the stream to emerge from the park at 4.9 miles and connect with a fire road that leads left in another mile to VA612 that's out of Crimora to the west.

Skyline Drive: From the Riprap Hollow Overlook at Mile 91.4, you'll overlook Riprap Hollow with Wildcat Ridge to the left.

At the Moormans River Overlook at Mile 92.0, you can see the reservoir for Charlottesville to the southeast. The reservoir lies on the Moormans River, where the North and South Forks come together. The Moorman family settled land in the area of the river in the early 1700s.

74 Wildcat Ridge Trail

2.7 miles one-way
Moderate
Elevation loss: 1300 ft.
Cautions: Stream crossings
Connections: Appalachian Trail, Riprap Trail

Attractions: This trail with the Riprap Trail and the AT forms a good loop hike.

Trailhead: Stop at the Wildcat Ridge Parking Area on the west side of Skyline Drive at Mile 92.1.

Description: The Wildcat Ridge Trail descends from the parking area to cross the AT at 0.1 mile. To the left, the AT reaches Jarman Gap in 5.8 miles. To the right the AT leads to Riprap Parking in 2.7 miles. The Riprap Trail, Wildcat Ridge Trail, and the AT can be used for a loop hike of 9.3 miles.

Continue straight down the Wildcat Ridge Trail. You'll dip through a sag at 0.4 mile and then continue down the ridge. The trail curves left at 1.1 miles as it descends across a south-facing slope with a profusion of mountain laurel that blooms in May and June. Switchback right in the descent.

You'll follow a small hollow down in a steep descent to rockhop a tributary stream of Riprap Hollow at 2.0 miles. On the other side, the trail turns left to follow the creek downstream along an old roadway. You'll pass small pools in the stream where you can dangle your feet on a hot summer day. At 2.3 miles, the trail leaves the old roadway to the right and switchbacks down to another rockhop of the stream at 2.4 miles as you descend farther into Riprap Hollow.

At 2.6 miles, you'll ford the main stream in Riprap Hollow and ascend to a junction with the Riprap Trail at 2.7 miles. To the left on the Riprap Trail you'd reach the park boundary in 0.9 mile. To the right, the trail leads 3.6 miles up to the AT where you'd turn south to reach the Riprap Parking Area in another 0.4 mile.

Skyline Drive: At Mile 92.4, the AT crosses Skyline Drive; there's parking on the west side.

At Crimora Lake Overlook at Mile 92.6, you'll have a view west with Turk Mountain to the far left and Wildcat Ridge to the right in front of Rocks Mountain. Down from the overlook, you'll look toward the community of Crimora where mining for manganese began in the 1860s and continued off and on until 1946; the manganese was used with iron in the making of steel. During World War II, the Crimora Mine produced more manganese than any other mining operation in the U.S. The mine is thought to be named after a young woman. You'll see two lakes associated with the mine operation. Crimora Lake lies directly out from the overlook in among trees; it's hard to spot because the water is black, but maybe you'll catch the sun shining on the water surface. A small stream was dammed to create the lake in 1915 to supply water for washing the ore. To the left, you'll see a blue-green lake that is a water-filled mine pit.

At the Turk Mountain Overlook at Mile 93.7, you'll look southwest to Turk Mountain where exposed Erwin quartzite makes a slash across the top of the mountain; it looks like a road-cut, but it is in fact a natural feature.

75 Turk Mountain Trail

1.1 miles one-way
Moderate
Elevation gain: 300 ft.
Cautions: Talus slopes
Connections: AT, Turk Branch Trail, Turk Gap Trail

Attractions: You'll have a good view north from the summit of Turk Mountain.

Trailhead: You'll find parking on the east in Turk Gap at Mile 94.1; the AT crosses the Drive. On the east, the AT heads north to Wildcat Ridge Parking in 2.2 miles. Also on the east, the Turk Branch Trail to the right follows an old road down the mountain 2.5 miles to connect with the South Fork of the Moormans River Fire Road. Walk across the Drive to pick up the AT on the west, headed south. The Turk Gap Trail, off to the right, follows an old road down the mountain to the park boundary in 1.7 miles.

Description: Follow the AT down to the left. You'll pass through pine and laurel to reach a junction at 0.1 mile with the Turk Mountain Trail to the right. The AT continues straight toward Jarman Gap in 3.6 miles. Turn right on the Turk Mountain Trail.

The trail drops through a saddle, passes over a rise, and then begins the ascent of Turk Mountain at 0.4 mile. You'll cross talus slopes and then switchback right and left up through rocks at 0.9 mile. The trail reaches the ridgeline and turns right up to the rocky summit of Turk Mountain at 1.1 miles (2981 ft.). Keep going up through the rocks to get to a great view north and west.

Skyline Drive: The AT crosses the Drive at the north end of the Sawmill Run Overlook at Mile 95.3. Sawmill Run lies below the overlook with the two summits of Calf Mountain to the left and Sawmill Ridge and Turk Mountain to the right.

You'll have virtually the same view from the Sawmill Ridge Overlook at Mile 95.9. Across the Drive, you'll find a good exposure of the sandstone, quartzite, and phyllite of the Weverton for-

View from Turk Mountain

mation, mostly rust-colored from iron deposits.

At Mile 96.1, Gasline Road descends the west side of the mountain to emerge from the park and connect with VA611/622. The road was built for a gas pipeline; access is limited.

The Drive passes through Jarman Gap at Mile 96.8; Thomas Jarman owned the gap in the early 1800s. You can access the AT by roads on the east. The South Fork of the Moormans River Fire Road to the left heads north toward the Charlottesville Reservoir. The Bucks Elbow Road to the right branches to the left at the park boundary to head up Bucks Elbow Mountain to a radio tower; the road's right branch continues down the mountain as VA611.

From Jarman Gap, the AT heads south to leave the park and reach the PATC Calf Mountain Hut in 1.0 mile and the summit of Calf Mountain in 1.6 miles. From Jarman Gap south, the park boundary is not much more than Skyline Drive; the AT travels outside the park. The park once ended at Jarman Gap but in 1961 was extended south to Rockfish Gap.

At the Calf Mountain Overlook on the west at Mile 98.9, you can see Waynesboro below with Scott and Bear Den Mountains to the left and Sawmill Ridge and Turk Mountain to the right.

The AT crosses the Drive in Beagle Gap at Mile 99.5; to the north it's a mile to the summit of Calf Mountain. From the Beagle Gap Overlook at Mile 99.8, Greenwood Hollow leads to the Piedmont on the east. The AT crosses the Drive in McCormick Gap at Mile 102.1. Below McCormick Gap Overlook at Mile 102.4 lies Sawmill Run valley with Sawmill Ridge on the left. The nearby mountain on the right with the radio towers is Bear Den Mountain.

At Mile 104.6 stands the Rockfish Gap Entrance Station. The AT comes down from the east to join the Drive at Mile 105.2 and stays on the road to cross US250 and I-64 in Rockfish Gap at Mile 105.4. The early passage through Rockfish Gap became a turnpike in 1808; Mountain Top Hotel and Leakes Tavern were located in the gap. A railroad tunnel runs under the mountain.

In Rockfish Gap, you have left Shenandoah National Park. Although Skyline Drive ends, the scenic highway continues south as the Blue Ridge Parkway 469 miles to the Great Smoky Mountain National Park.

Selected References

Appenzelter, Tim, "Travels of America," *Discover,* September 1996, pp.80-87.

Conners, John A. 1988. *Shenandoah National Park, An Interpretive Guide.* Blacksburg, Va.: The McDonald & Woodward Publishing Company.

Floyd, Tom. 1981. *Lost Trails and Forgotten People, The Story of Jones Mountain.* Vienna, Va.: The Potomac Appalachian Trail Club.

Gathright II, Thomas M. 1976. *Geology of the Shenandoah National Park, Virginia.* Charlottesville: Virginia Division of Mineral Resources.

Gupton, Oscar W., and Fred C. Swope. 1981. *Trees and Shrubs of Virginia.* Charlottesville: University Press of Virginia.

Gupton, Oscar W., and Fred C. Swope. 1979. *Wildflowers of the Shenandoah Valley and Blue Ridge Mountains.* Charlottesville: University Press of Virginia.

Heatwole, Henry. 1978, updated 1990. *Guide to Shenandoah National Park and Skyline Drive.* Luray, Va.: Shenandoah Natural History Association.

Lambert, Darwin. 1989. *The Undying Past of Shenandoah National Park.* Boulder, Co.: Roberts Rinehart, Inc. Publishers.

Lambert, Darwin. 1971. *Herbert Hoover's Hideaway.* Luray, Va.: Shenandoah Natural History Association.

Mazzeo, Peter M. 1986. *Trees of Shenandoah National Park.* Luray, Va.: Shenandoah Natural History Association.

Pollock, George Freeman. 1960. *Skyland: The Heart of the Shenandoah National Park.* Chesapeake Book Company.

Reeder, Carolyn and Jack. 1991. *Shenandoah Secrets, The Story of the Park's Hidden Past.* Vienna, Va.: The Potomac Appalachian Trail Club.

Reeder, Carolyn and Jack. 1980. *Shenandoah Vestiges: What the Mountain People Left Behind.* Vienna, Va.: The Potomac Appalachian Trail Club.

Reeder, Carolyn and Jack. 1978. *Shenandoah Heritage, The Story of the People Before the Park.* Vienna, Va.: The Potomac Appalachian Trail Club.

Stanley, Steven M. 1986. *Earth and Life Through Time.* New York: W. H. Freeman and Co.

Stoneberger, John W. 1993. *Memories of a Lewis Mountain Man.* Vienna, Va.: The Potomac Appalachian Trail Club.

Trail Index

Hiking

Horse

Addresses & Phone Numbers

ARAMARK Shenandoah
National Park Lodges
P.O. Box 727
Luray, VA 22835
800/999-4714

Graves' Mountain Lodge
Route 670
Syria, VA 22743-9999
540/923-4231

Heritage House B&B
P.O. Box 427
Washington, VA 22747
540/675-3207

Jordon Hollow Farm
Rt. 2 Box 375
Stanley, VA, 22851
540/778-2285

Potomac Appalachian Trail Club
118 Park Street, SE
Vienna, VA 22180-4609
703/242-0315
Monday -Thursday 7:00 pm-
9:00 pm
Thursday-Friday 12:00 noon-
2:00 pm

Shenandoah National Park
Rt. 4 Box 348
Luray, VA 22835
540/999-3500

Shenandoah Natural History
Association
3655 US Hwy. 211E
Luray, VA 22835-9036
540/999-3582

The Mayne View
439 Mechanic Street
Luray, VA 22835
540/743-7921

The Mimslyn
401 W. Main St.
Luray, VA 22835
800/296-5105

Woodward House on Manor
Grade
413 South Royal Avenue
Front Royal, VA 22630
800/635-7011

Other Books and Maps
from Mountain Laurel Place

Maps of Shenandoah
We've blown up the trail maps in this book, *The Best of Shenandoah*, to 8 1/2 x 11 inches to show more detail. 10 maps. $4.95

The Best of the Great Smoky Mountains
A hiker's guide to trails and attractions of the Great Smoky Mountains National Park of Tennessee and North Carolina. 256 pp., photos, maps. $10.95

Trails of the Big South Fork
A complete guide for hikers, mountain bikers, and horse riders to the trails of the Big South Fork National River and Recreation Area of Tennessee and Kentucky. 256 pp., photos, maps. $12.95

Exploring the Big South Fork
A complete handbook to the geology, biology, and history of the Big South Fork National River and Recreation Area plus many details on outdoor activities, including hiking, horseback riding, paddling, and mountain biking. 240 pp., color and B&W photos, maps. $15.95

Tennessee's South Cumberland
A hiker's guide to trails and attractions of Tennessee's South Cumberland Recreation Area, Fall Creek Falls and Cumberland Mountain State Parks, Franklin and Prentice Cooper State Forests, plus several natural areas and pocket wildernesses. 135 pp., photos, maps. $8.95

The Historic Cumberland Plateau
(published by the University of Tennessee Press)
An explorer's guide to the history and the outdoors of the Cumberland Plateau in Tennessee, Kentucky, and Alabama, providing historical background and giving specific directions on how to explore the region. 360 pp., photos, maps. $14.95

Historic Knoxville and Knox County
(Bicentennial Edition)
A walking and touring guide to the historic city center, neighborhoods, parks, and back roads of this Tennessee city and county. 256 pp., photos, maps. $4.95 (Regular $8.95)

214

Appalachian Trail Guide to Shenandoah National Park
(published by The Potomac Appalachian Trail Club)
A detailed guide to the AT through Shenandoah National Park and brief descriptions of side trails. 352 pp., 3 foldout maps. $21.95

Map 9 North District, Map 10 Central District, Map 11 South District
AT and Other Trails in Shenandoah National Park
(published by The Potomac Appalachian Trail Club)
Topographical maps showing road and trails in Shenandoah National Park. $5.95 each

Map 228, Shenandoah National Park, Virginia
(published by Trails Illustrated)
A topographical map showing roads and trails in the entire Shenandoah National Park. Waterproof, tearproof. $8.99

Guide to Massanutten Mountain
(published by The Potomac Appalachian Trail Club)
A guide to 40 trails on Massanutten Mountain within George Washington National Forest. Massanutten stands in Shenandoah Valley and can be seen to the west from Skyline Drive in Shenandoah National Park. 74 pp., maps. $5.95

A Cyclist's Guide to Shenandoah Valley
(published by Shenandoah Odysseys)
Two-wheel travel on quiet backroads through the farmland and forests of Shenandoah Valley. 200 pp., maps and photos. $14.95

Hiking Virginia's National Forests
(published by Globe Pequot Press)
A guide to hiking trails in the national forests in the state of Virginia. 176 pp., maps and photos. $9.95

The Hiker's Guide to Virginia
(published by Falcon Press)
A sampling of hikes in the state of Virginia. 168 pp., maps and photos. $12.95

Order Form

Send check or money order to:

Mountain Laurel Place

P.O. Box 3001

Norris, TN 37828

Telephone & fax

423/494-8121

Title	Price	Quantity	Total
Best of Shenandoah	$12.95		
Maps of Shenandoah	$ 4.95		
Best of the Great Smoky Mtns.	$10.95		
Trails of the Big South Fork	$12.95		
Exploring the Big South Fork	$15.95		
Tennessee's South Cumberland	$ 8.95		
The Historic Cumberland Plateau	$16.95		
Historic Knoxville & Knox Co.	$ 4.95		
AT Guide to Shenandoah NP	$21.95		
Map 9. SNP North District	$ 5.95		
Map 10. SNP Central District	$ 5.95		
Map 11. SNP South District	$ 5.95		
Map 228. Shenandoah NP	$ 8.99		
Cyclist's Guide to Shen. Valley	$14.95		
Guide to Massanutten Mtn.	$ 5.95		
Hiking VA's National Forests	$ 9.95		
Hiker's Guide to Virginia	$12.95		
Subtotal			
Tenn. residents add 8.25% sales tax			
Shipping and handling*			
Total enclosed			

*Add $2.00 for shipping/handling if ordering one item or for each item if separate mailing is requested. **We pay for shipping/handling if more than one item is ordered and mailed in one shipment to the same the address.**

Ship to ───────────────────────

Address ───────────────────────

───────────────────────

Items offered subject to availability. Prices subject to change without notice.